Internal Communication in the Age of Artificial Intelligence

Internal Communication in the Age of Artificial Intelligence

Monique Zytnik

Internal Communication in the Age of Artificial Intelligence

Copyright © Business Expert Press, LLC, 2024

Cover design by Jan Tredop, Berlin, Germany
Author photo by Heike Niemeier, Berlin, Germany

Interior design by Exeter Premedia Services Private Ltd., Chennai, India

All rights reserved. No part of this publication may be reproduced, stored in a retrieval system, or transmitted in any form or by any means—electronic, mechanical, photocopy, recording, or any other except for brief quotations, not to exceed 400 words, without the prior permission of the publisher.

First published in 2024 by
Business Expert Press, LLC
222 East 46th Street, New York, NY 10017
www.businessexpertpress.com

ISBN-13: 978-1-63742-604-3 (paperback)
ISBN-13: 978-1-63742-605-0 (e-book)

Business Expert Press Corporate Communication Collection

First edition: 2024

10 9 8 7 6 5 4 3 2 1

With thanks to my family who have provided me with unfailing support in completing my passion project.

Description

Transformational Leaders Need to Be Exceptional Communicators

Bombarded by new technology and unsure where artificial intelligence will take us? Asking yourself how this will impact communication at scale in your organization? How can you best harness this power for business success?

Companies and projects are at risk. Effective strategic internal communication will attract, engage, align, and retain your people to weather this storm of change. It will also help them adopt new technologies and be a part of the transformation.

But how can you tell if your strategy will succeed? What questions should you ask?

Internal Communication in the Age of Artificial Intelligence reveals a modern, multilayered approach to internal communication. It's a practical guide for business leaders and communicators, filled with global case studies, behind-the-scenes insights, and stories from industry experts. You'll learn what basics must be done brilliantly, how to engage with communities, and why a new immersive communication mindset is needed to prepare you for the future.

Keywords

internal communication; internal communication strategy; strategic internal communication; leadership communication; innovative internal communication; employee experience; employer branding; corporate communication; immersive technology; organizational communication; employee communications; strategic alignment model; multilayered internal communication model

Contents

Testimonials xi
Disclaimer xv
Foreword xvii
Preface xix
Acknowledgments xxv
Introduction: Living in a World of Change xxvii

Chapter 1: Good, Better, Best Strategic Internal Communication 1
Chapter 2: Content Is King, Strategy Is Queen 21
Chapter 3: Foundation: The Basics You Can't Miss 37
Chapter 4: Multidirectional Networks 61
Chapter 5: Immersive Communication 77
Chapter 6: Leadership Communication 99
Chapter 7: Strategic Alignment and Activating Your Team 115
Chapter 8: Embracing Tomorrow 131

Bibliography 139
About the Author 147
Index 149

Testimonials

"We need to reimagine a more human-centered and sustainable way of conducting business. One that combines the advantages of emerging technology with the uniquely human strengths that we can all bring to the table. *Internal Communication in the Age of Artificial Intelligence* shows how, despite new technology and new ways of working, building relationships, communicating effectively, and promoting strong, purpose-driven leadership is what matters, and will continue to matter. Monique's engaging way of looking at internal communication and her multilayered model gives us a pathway to a more human-centric future and positions organizational communication as one of the essential tools to navigate the complexity and disruption to come. An essential thought-provoking read." —**Aaron McEwan, VP, Research & Advisory, Gartner, Sydney, Australia**

"*Internal Communication in the Age of Artificial Intelligence* is a testimonial to the transformative power of IABC's global IABC network of thought leaders and communication experts. In this book, Monique draws on her multifaceted experience in corporations and as a consultant to educate readers about the potential of generative AI in enabling (not replacing) human-centered communication. Through an engaging storytelling format, Monique takes us inside her world, drawing upon theory and practical examples to illustrate internal communication effectiveness in today's and future AI-powered business environments. I highly recommend this book to leaders and communication professionals." —**Maliha Aqeel, International Association of Business Communicators (IABC) Global Board Chair, Toronto, Canada**

"*Internal Communication in the Age of Artificial Intelligence by Monique Zytnik is a must-read for business leaders and communicators. The book explores the impact of AI on internal communication and provides practical insights, useful global case studies, expert opinions—as well as links to great podcasts. Monique Zytnik uses compelling storytelling to emphasize the *importance of effective internal communication for business success and discusses the challenges and opportunities presented by new AI technology. The book is well-written, lively, and informative and provides a modern, multilayered approach to internal communication. A really valuable resource for anyone looking to improve their internal communication strategy and impact in the age of AI."* —**Morten Dal, Change Management & Customer Success Management, Microsoft, Copenhagen, Denmark**

"What an entertaining read! Filled with real stories, real case studies, great interviews with industry experts and practical models, Monique helps show what great internal communication looks like. This book is essential for any leader wanting to make an impact at scale in their organization.

AI is here to stay and every leader needs to be aware of the risks and opportunities. Internal Communication in the Age of Artificial Intelligence *should sit at the top of your must-read books."* —**Gabrielle Dolan, international keynote speaker and author of *Magnetic Stories*, Melbourne, Australia**

"With so many opinions on offer today about where better communications can help your organization, this book is a great guide to the forest. It explains why internal communications matters—now and in the future. Importantly, highly experienced practitioner Monique explains enduring truths about the importance of strategic thinking and the need to understand audiences; she avoids the trap of talking about individual tools or gone tomorrow technologies but rather highlights the need to remember the WHY and the WHO of communication.

This book reflects a wealth of research drawing on academic research, insights from real practitioners, and some of the most influential management thinkers of our age. Monique's global mindset is reflected in the sources she draws up and her pithy writing style ensures that her aphorisms will be with us for a long time to come." —**Liam FitzPatrick, Coauthor of *Successful Employee Communications*, London, United Kingdom**

"The most successful leaders possess effective communication skills, which help them build trust by leading authentically. In this must-read book, Monique guides leaders on how to use this power on a large scale to create value. It's

smart and engaging. She uses entertaining stories and case studies to explain what good internal communication looks like and how leadership and strategic alignment play a vital role. Best yet, she provides leaders with valuable questions to help them get the best counsel and support from their communication experts and prepares them for the uncertain future that AI brings."
—**David Grossman, leadership and communication expert, and author of the award-winning book,** *Heart First: Lasting Leader Lessons from the Year that Changed Everything,* **Chicago, United States of America**

"As the head of strategy at a leading communication planning network, I am blown away by Monique and her book, Internal Communication in the Age of Artificial Intelligence. *While we find ourselves heading into a world where AI is bound to have an impact on almost everything around us, we ought to remember that AI is after all just an enabler. Monique effectively emphasizes this while showing us practical ways to bring together the power of technology and the essence of human-centric communication strategies. The frameworks and action points that she has laid out are rooted in prioritizing the human touch while being applicable to a wide range of use cases. They are also vital for any organization that aims to deliver contextually relevant internal communications that align to their broader marketing goals, while also consistently connecting with their audiences, both internal and external.*

"People come first. Technology merely enables"—these words of wisdom from Monique should well and truly be a mantra for anyone in the corporate world as we get ready to embrace the future." —**Kiron Kesav, Chief Strategy Officer, Omnicom Media Group, Kuala Lumpur, Malaysia**

"As managing partners at the Center for Strategic Communication Excellence, we've witnessed firsthand the indispensable role internal communication plays in driving organizational success. Internal Communication in the Age of Artificial Intelligence *presents a thought-provoking examination of how AI can seamlessly integrate into internal communication practices at a time where technological advancements are rapidly transforming how we connect. Monique offers a compelling narrative on harnessing AI to enhance, rather than replace, the human-centered approach that lies at the core of effective communication. For communication professionals seeking to elevate*

their strategic influence, Monique's insights are an invaluable asset." —**Sia Papageorgiou and Adrian Cropley, Managing Partners, Center for Strategic Communication Excellence (CSCE), Melbourne, Australia**

"Monique's multilayered internal communication model sets out the thinking that we need to be adopting right now for the future. She skillfully builds on existing internal communication theory, adding a new layer that touches on the human-focused, experiential and immersive communication that is emerging. Her book is a pivotal piece that helps not only our practitioners but also the leaders we need to influence, understand what great internal communication looks like, regardless of the technology they have at their fingertips. It's an essential addition to your business book collection." —**Jennifer Sproul, Chief Executive, Institute of Internal Communication, Milton Keynes, United Kingdom**

"George Bernard Shaw aptly summed it up, "the single biggest problem in communication is the illusion that it has taken place." Today's modern leadership relies on communication and importantly comprehension to harness efforts and achieve goals.

Monique's take on Leadership Communication in her latest book explores just this, and emphasizes consistency, strategic storytelling, and personal branding as being the cornerstones for inspiring and effecting meaningful change.

Internal Communication in the Age of Artificial Intelligence is a compelling call to action for leaders and communicators alike to forge genuine connections, build trust, and lead with integrity in an era where such values hold more meaning than ever." —**Harsh Vardhan, Investor Relations Senior Executive, Abu Dhabi Commercial Bank (ADCB), Abu Dhabi Emirate, United Arab Emirates**

Disclaimer

This book is largely based on human effort, with real people, real names, and real stories. They flew through my fingers onto the keyboard. Artificial intelligence (AI) was used for initial ideation and later for grammar suggestions. Speech recognition was used to quickly convert audio recordings to text for my interviews. My cover design is the perfect representation of how AI should work. My designer Jan Tredop used Midjourney to generate the people graphic, which he then tweaked in Photoshop to create the final image.

Foreword

Reflecting over my years, one of my proudest achievements was cofounding and running Gatehouse, a renowned internal communication consultancy to the point of selling to Gallagher—a global insurance and professional services company, and being able to retire well ahead of the game. I'd spent a couple of decades in the ever-changing industry of internal communication, worked with some of the world's biggest brands such as the BBC, EY, HSBC, GSK, and the World Health Organization, to name but a few, and established State of the Sector as one of the leading global industry reports. My time with internal communication was officially over! I had planned to spend the year 2020 traveling across the British Isles to visit each of the 400+ islands and maybe write another book or make a podcast, but the world had different ideas.

As I and pretty much everyone else were forced indoors for huge chunks of time, I began looking back at my career and started to miss my old life. The roller coaster of days dealing with client challenges, the interesting people I met, and the constant rigor of running a fast-paced global consultancy began gnawing at my now, largely sedentary life. As 2021 rolled in, I was asked to step back into the world I vowed I had left. Open Communication Group, a global internal communication consultancy, invited me to take up the position as their chair.

Dusting down my internal communication clothes, I began the return to my old life; except postpandemic, as with most things, it had changed dramatically. The rise of technology had now meant that I, as the only member of the team based in the United Kingdom, was in daily video conversations with my colleagues in Denmark and South Africa, from the comfort of my home.

As I began introducing myself to various team members, an e-mail popped up from a colleague to remind me that we also had a base in Berlin, Germany, and suggested that it might be nice to meet. I was delighted to do so. We began a series of regular conversations—whether about work, the industry, offering strategic advice, or simply just chatting.

And that is how I first met Monique Zytnik—a co-worker, a networker, who, over a relatively short period, became a friend.

It wasn't, however, until I was asked to write the foreword to this excellent book, that I had any idea that Monique's career started in medicine! To take the learnings and experience from a sector that, on face value would seem so far away from the world of internal communication and make such an impactful transition, is a testament to her knowledge, insights, and natural capability.

Fast forward just two years from our first meeting, Monique has become one of the industry's shining lights. When we first talked about how earlier in her career she'd wanted to test herself by presenting at conferences, to the Monique I know today, who is in regular demand to share her significant experiences to ever larger audiences, I've had the pleasure of witnessing her flourish as one of the preeminent influencers as well as becoming a recognized expert in the particularly relevant and very current subject of artificial intelligence. Her work with some of the world's largest organizations has brought with it a knowledge that few possess, and her generosity in sharing the many stories and case studies she has captured along the way is a valuable resource in itself.

So when Monique asked if I would write her foreword, I was truly honored. It did mean, of course, that I would have to read her book, and as Monique is very aware, having spent most of my adult life reading and writing laborious content, I have avoided actually reading a book from choice, for over a decade—but what a great way to break that seal! This is one of the most readable texts I've had the pleasure of sitting down with. She asked me for comments and feedback. I had none. This is not your standard textbook. You will very quickly forget that this is a book of learning and devour its contents in the same way you might a thriller or other such genre. It is very much a page-turner.

So, if you want to better understand the future of internal communication in the age of AI, but also get to know Monique Zytnik a little better along the way, then get stuck in. I'm confident you will walk away feeling informed, nervous/excited for the future and energized. Enjoy!

—Simon Wright

Preface

I fell into internal communication by lucky accident.

My high school scores got me into medicine, but I couldn't stand the sight of blood. So, I trained and qualified as a physiotherapist.[*] I loved the classes in anatomy and dissection, massage, research methods, and biomechanics, especially the academic and practical scientific methodology behind physiotherapy. The process involved asking questions, looking at objective data and observations, assessing the problem, and then putting together a practical, manageable plan.

It wasn't until I was a practicing physio that I realized the profession wasn't for me.

What they didn't teach us at university was that success was often based on something more than just science. It was about the complexities of the whole person and not just the knee, ankle, or hip. I became disenchanted with my profession when I realized I could tell the day my patient decided to get better. It was all about effective communication, persuasion, and persistence.

Physiotherapy is usually a slow and painful process, no matter what treatment you prescribe, unless the patient wants to change, get better, and they understand what they need to do. The idea that it wasn't all about hard science or numbers fascinated me, and I became known for getting great results with complex patients.

I once had a particularly challenging patient with hypersensitivity; even fabric against her skin could cause her pain. She was born with a foot deformity, and when I met her, she was in a large, black electric wheelchair, almost the size of a tiny car. With the levers, springy seat, and chunky wheels, it just about needed a car license to maneuver through the outpatient clinic. Over a few weeks, I gradually built up her strength, persuading her to use the therapy pool and encouraging her to go further.

---

[*] Often known as a physical therapist in the United States.

A lot of what I did was try to understand her as a person including her fears and motivations, and practice good communication skills.

While treating this patient, I learned a second important lesson—everything is ultimately about business, about getting results that bring in money. I remember feeling a deep, visceral outrage when management told us to discharge her because her insurance funding had run out. Making money was what ran the hospital. She was back in intensive care at another hospital shortly afterward, then back to us. We got more funding, and I left the profession.

Understanding business is essential to workplace success. Influencing and operating within it is essential to your success.

The art of persuasion intrigued me, and my postgraduate diploma in public relations from RMIT University in Melbourne had me applying strategy to media relations, content marketing, and event management. I interned in public relations at an American consultancy in Washington, DC, less than six months after the September 11 attacks. It was a different era. The Internet was on the rise, social media was just around the corner, and online dating had become acceptable.

Back in Australia, I also worked for Australia's multilingual public broadcaster, Special Broadcasting Services (SBS), the state and federal governments, and even an intensive care charity, building on my understanding of marketing, public relations, and communication theory.

Then, a good friend told me about her work as an internal communication professional. I found it fascinating that someone could have a job simply helping people understand what was happening in their organization. As a physio, I'd seen a big disconnect between what management thinks and what staff understands. At other workplaces working in marketing and public relations, I'd also observed that the water cooler conversation was more valuable than anything you'd receive officially. But when I entered the profession, I had no idea that it wielded so much power and could have such an impact on organizational results.

Internal communication professionals are ultimately responsible for information flow within their organization. They need to present the CEO in a way that inspires people to follow, position the C-suite, help staff understand and live the culture, align people at all levels with the corporate agenda, support managers with team communication … The list goes on.

My career in pure internal communications began in a contract role at ANZ Bank in Melbourne just before the global financial crisis. It was a new experience for me when I discovered how important good communication within a company is for the happiness and health of its employees. Internal communication professionals were partnered with human resource (HR) professionals during offshoring projects; repetitive jobs were moved to cheaper labor markets overseas. Planning this out and making sure that employees were communicated with respectfully were huge responsibilities. The experience was also a sign of what was coming with artificial intelligence (AI).

When I started learning about communication at scale in 2002, the theory was almost wholly based on the sender–receiver model. Later on, when I completed my master's degree in Communications in 2010, this was still the case. As Facebook and social media platforms became more mainstream during this time, there became more of a focus on building communities and networks.

Now, I see a new shift that is well underway.

A smart technology revolution is upon us. New and advanced concepts such as the metaverse, augmented reality, hybrid work, and AI have rapidly transformed how businesses communicate with their employees.

Through my work with these new technologies, I saw that our communication models need a refresh. The basics still hold, but more is needed. Rapidly changing tech brings new challenges, and the basic principles for internal communication are still being missed.

I'm tired of decision makers who unthinkingly accept familiar strategies from past campaigns without considering changed circumstances or understanding the underlying strategy. I've seen too many campaigns cookie-cut from previous campaigns. Leaders with their standard toolbox of townhall meeting followed up by an e-mail—and that's it. No further support to help embed the concept, no listening to understand the issues or tailored communication to address specific groups. AI can help improve the quality of content or produce it faster, but without the skills to know what is good and accurate, there is a risk that too much content is produced. The time and resource costs that historically have restricted the quantity of content won't be there to help limit how much content is published. Employees may become overwhelmed with content if the creators do not understand context and strategy. I use the word creators here because you no longer need to be a professional communicator to create content.

Content may be king, but strategy is queen, with more moves and distance. It is hard to win on a king alone.

And, while some people say culture eats strategy for breakfast, I'd say that communication breathes life into the culture, and without being strategic about it, you'd have a meager breakfast. A confusing mess.

We must be thoughtful about adding more layers into our communication toolbox to give us more flexibility. We need to build on what we have to communicate effectively with our people of all levels within an organization.

This book brings together strategic concepts in an easy-to-apply model. I've taken a timeless approach to technology because I know how fast products evolve in the marketplace. For example, I refer to enterprise social networks (ESNs) instead of the Microsoft product Yammer because products and names are changing increasingly quickly. In 2023, Yammer's name was changed to Viva Engage, a perfect example of a big brand product with remarkably short name longevity. It's hard to keep up.

It's easy to say, well, a book is old-fashioned; why didn't you create a metaverse to explain your story? My answer is, I did. My colleagues and I created one for the International Association of Business Communicators (IABC) World Conference in June 2021, where Andreas Ringsted and I presented in a virtual space with a client and case study. There is even a terrible YouTube video of me getting excited about the different levels in my three-layered model, waving my arms around, and Andreas next to me looking calm with his deadpan Nordic Viking face barely showing a hint of a smile. I like to tease him. Like me, Andreas loves ideas, debating, working out best practices, and, most of all, sharing, just because ideas are great and lead to great things. And when he cracks a smile, you know it.

So, to add that immersive element throughout this book, I've added QR codes and links to multimedia content to delve into and add that desirable layer of richness.

Finally, I am relieved to see, or at least start to get the impression, that employee experience is on par with customer experience in the minds of our organizational leaders and decision makers. Gradually, there is an increasing awareness that employee experience leads to the customer experience, which leads to profit (or loss). However, many organizations and countries still have a long way to go.

There is also a pleasing trend toward recognizing that internal communication is also external, that employees are also customers and potential advocates and a way to reach even larger audiences. Employer branding is now confidently paired with internal communication, bridging the employee experience gap from external marketing in the recruitment phase, right through the employee life cycle to the alumni phase. In our never-ending war on talent, internal communication has now earned its seat at the table as a part of the solution.

I know that these themes are on the minds of many senior leaders in communication and increasingly at the C-suite level when looking at organizational efficiency. I work with these people daily. At heart, I am a practical person. I dislike inefficiency and noise creation that distracts people in our organizations. I'm also not fond of time, resources, and money wasted on ineffective campaigns that don't achieve results.

As technological advancement is speeding ahead, I see the opportunity for our leaders and communication professionals to become more strategic and discerning about what they do and how they do it to ensure our organizations are healthy, effective workplaces.

Money may be the driver, but success comes through the people.

Acknowledgments

When you stand up and have something to say, butterflies can easily come fast surrounding you and suffocating you. But when you look out and reach out and see all the people who you value standing by your side, listening, and cheering you on, the butterflies transform into exhilarating energy.

Thank you to each and every person who has given their time and shared their wisdom with me for this book. You'll see some of their names and stories throughout. To my networks within the IABC, Institute of Internal Communication (IoIC), Global Women in Public Relations (GWPR), European Association of Communication Directors (EACD), The Mentoring Club, and Kelly Irving's Expert Author Community, thanks for cheering me on. And to my book reviewers, Anton Zytnik, Carine Chisu, Daven Rosener, Pete Carvill, Rosie Mowatt, and Ross Monaghan, feedback is a gift. Thank you for your expertise and insights.

To my friend and designer, Nicole Nicolaus, your "beautification" of everything you work with always leaves me in awe. Thank you for bringing my model life.

My gratitude goes to Scott Isenberg, Charlene Kronstedt, and the team at Business Expert Press. Ideas are exciting and a book should be a pleasure to read.

Introduction: Living in a World of Change

What's on Your Mind?

"What's top of my mind is AI," Sean said. "But no one in our organization seems to be thinking about it, thinking about the long-term implications."

The sun was blinding bright in my eyes, even though my sunglasses were perched on my nose. I could feel a trickle of sweat crawling down between my shoulder blades as the late Melbourne summer finally arrived. I didn't mind the heat, as it was lovely to be outside, in a social setting, talking to my manager about big-picture ideas.

Over the years, I've become used to meeting with people remotely, staring at them through the screen with my headset on, and talking with them across Australia, or between different countries. Now, more than ever, I treasure real-life, in-person moments and conversations, even though there are colleagues and clients I've collaborated effectively with and never met.

I could hear the bubbly noise of the people seated around me, chatting at the café next to our office. Others were standing, lounging, and talking loudly in their flashy city outfits as they also took joy in meeting friends and work colleagues in person. No sign of home-office track pants here. The ice in my glass clinked as I sipped the cool water and put on my inquiring face.

Where to go from there, I thought. It's a big topic. AI covers so many things: so many opportunities and so many risks. Like many fellow leaders and communication professionals, I knew Sean was interested in the content creation abilities of different platforms that can spit out written content in seconds or generate custom images with the right request. Sure, the content could sometimes be dubious and needed to be fact-checked, but it wasn't bad for a quick artificial brain dump. Friends of mine have been playing with different generative AI (GenAI) programs to draft content marketing, using it as an ideation tool for a campaign or to help them develop a rough strategy. I briefly thought of some of the draft articles new graduates had produced for me, the hours it had taken them, and how many revisions I'd needed to work through with them to help with their learning process, and I winced.

"We need to bring people together across the organization to look at this together; there are so many opportunities and risks," I said cautiously, warming up to the topic. I peered through my sunglasses, leaned forward, and paused. "I think we need to look at where communication, internal communicators, can now be creating impact."

"And what about our people in our organizations? How will it impact them?" I mused. Content is cheap. Change is fast. How will we take our people on the journey?

An Age of Artificial Intelligence

Since ChatGPT was released on the market in November 2022, conversations like this have occurred worldwide. We have all been mulling over what the future will bring. Some of us have also been tasting the excitement of what could be, while others have been fearful or just not interested in getting started anytime soon. This spectrum is reflected in the different levels of AI adoption maturity where some organizations are more advanced than others. From what I've seen in the past months, the smaller and more agile organizations have found it easier to play, learn, and adopt, whereas larger organizations have had many more committee processes and decision levels to go through to even start to look at possibilities.

Over the years, technology has changed the way we work. From the invention of the steam engine in 1804 to the almost daily improvements we're seeing in AI technology, it gives us new efficiency options and changes how we do things at work. And, we know that technology is developing exponentially faster than ever before.

But people don't tend to like rapid change. Over the coming years, we'll see more technology implementation and adoption projects, more pace of change, and a greater need for effective communication at work as we all deal with more complexity both in our personal and work-focused lives. There will be an ongoing tension between technology and humanity as technology moves faster than most people can change.

As we lurch from one trend to another and one shiny technology to another, AI has already changed, and will continue to change the way we work. AI is now a given in our lives. It is within this context that I write. This book is not about how to set up your internal communication using AI, but rather, given the new ways of working in our AI-powered environments, how can we best approach communicating at scale within our organizations to make sure we are getting business results and value. It will help you apply best practices in the best ways that suit you and your specific organization.

Communication With Employees at Scale

But why does professional organizational communication matter?

Internal communication is deliberate communication at scale with employees in your organization—from the C-suite to frontline staff—to support business goals. First and foremost, the purpose of internal communication is to make an organization successful. It is an integral enabler of business success.

FitzPatrick and Valskov in their book *Internal Communications: A Manual for Practitioners*, say that internal communications only adds value if there is a direct link to the needs of the business. Their number one rule is that it is about results and outcomes.

Today's main challenge is that most people believe they can communicate effectively because they can talk and write easily. I can see that the addition of new AI on this front could be both a help and a hindrance.

But communicating at scale is a more complex puzzle that needs additional skills than just ability related to the five senses. Organizational communication involves looking at the bigger picture and consciously crafting interactions to meet changing business needs.

To do this, one needs to be strategic and able to piece together the bigger jigsaw puzzle. You need to know where you are going and why you are doing something in order to work out the rest.

Many risks are inherent in poorly thought-out internal communication, such as creating noise that confuses staff who don't listen, understand, or care enough to engage with what you want them to do. For example, there is no need to publish separate internal news stories on safety, a leader profile, well-being, and mental health. An overall intranet news article connecting a leader's view on safety, both physical and mental, to the company's well-being policy, would streamline the experience for staff. Eye-catching photos and an optional audio file for those who want more detail could be used to better appeal to individual needs and interests.

You can waste staff members' time by giving them internal news that isn't relevant to them. You can also create dangerous situations where leaders aren't listening to crucial information from the frontline, impacting business decisions. For example, when the communication is poorly done in a merger, you can lose valuable staff and, unfortunately, retain low performers, whom you planned to make redundant anyway. Internal mishaps also go external, no matter how careful you are. Perhaps it's a clumsily worded leadership e-mail? A poorly communicated new policy on hybrid work? This can significantly impact your company's brand and reputation. Your customers, regulators, and potential new hires are certainly listening! Any experienced internal communication practitioner will tell you this based on their experience, based on best practice research.

Professor and Director of Internal Communication Research at the University of Florida's College of Journalism and Communication, Rita Men is unhesitant and unapologetic when she cites both her own and existing research evidence of the efficacy of a strategic approach to internal communication versus a more tactics-based approach. Her research has covered all aspects of internal communication including strategies, messaging channels, employee engagement, internal reputation, organizational relationships, internal crisis, leadership and anything else you could possibly imagine, with a strong focus on measurement evaluation. Her current research looks at how AI has been impacting public relations practice, including both the external and internal perspectives. Rita is also a consultant and blends this with practical client work. I spoke with her over a video call on September 29, 2023, after seeing a jaw-dropping number of her publications, copublished research papers, and books on the university's Internal Communication Research Hub. Rita had produced over 50 publications, and then I stopped counting.

"If it's managed strategically, we have research evidence showing internal communication is tied to employee outcomes," Rita explained. "Employee outcomes are measured from three levels, cognitive, affective, and behavioral."

Cognitive Employee Perceptions

The cognitive element is employees' perception or evaluation of the organization and the internal reputation of the organization. With excellent strategic internal communication, "they will rate the organization's internal reputation better and also they will perceive the organization being more transparent," Rita said. "They will perceive them being more authentic and they (the employees) identify more with their organization."

Affective Impact

The affective or relational outcomes of effective or strategic internal communication, include trust.

Rita said:

> If internal communication is done strategically and effectively, the employees tend to trust the organization more and they will be more satisfied and also more committed to working with the company instead of leaving for their competitors. They also have this feeling of empowerment—we call it control mutuality; it's a sense of shared control and empowerment. Trust helps the employees feel able to participate in decision making and competent to do the job they were assigned to do, impacting their overall happiness, mood, and emotions.

The Behavioral Impact of Strategic Internal Communication

On the behavioral level, Rita says the measurements used to demonstrate the effectiveness of internal communication including employee supportive behaviors such as employee voice behavior.

"They're more willing to share their concerns and their suggestions for the organization directly with their supervisors or the top management and also they are more willing to help one another in the organization," said Rita. "We call this organizational citizenship behavior. They are willing to walk actual miles beyond doing their normal duties and help the organization to be better."

Another desirable outcome is advocacy, which means employees are willing to protect the organization's reputation in times of crisis, in the face of external criticisms or as an active advocate; they are also willing to engage in positive word of mouth. They want to say good things about the company, on social media or offline among their friends. They will encourage people to work for this company and say it is an awesome company to work for, and you should come here, things like that.

Rita emphasizes that destructive behaviors resulting from poor or nonexistent internal communication need to be considered. These are the risks leaders face when doing nothing, or not investing. As a practitioner, I've observed destructive behavior and read 2023 research from the IoIC that supported this, but it was good to hear Rita's solid support of the idea.

"We also looked at some destructive behavior, for example, breaking the rules, stealing from the company, and having a negative association," Rita confirmed.

"If internal communication is done strategically and effectively, it can reduce those negative or destructive employee behaviors as well."

Employee Engagement

And then there's a lot of research showing the connection between employee engagement and financial performance productivity. "So it's tied to the bottom line of the organization," Rita said.

External Reputation

In today's social media era, the world is more transparent, and the line between internal and external is blurred. Anything internal could easily become external. Employees are their best ambassadors because they are credible sources of information. Compared with what the PR team says, or what the CEO says, the external public trusts employees more; so employees are the natural spokespeople. If your internal communication is effective, employees could become your best advocates, and strengthen the reputation of the company, which can increase sales, and potentially attract even more talent to the company. It ties to every aspect of the company's productivity, performance, and success.

"Those are some of the outcomes or measures we use to demonstrate the effectiveness of strategic internal communication," Rita concluded.

Excellent and competent internal communication matters to an organization and its leaders' success.

Who Are the Players in Our Futuristic Game?

Meet the stars in our story. We have Sean, the leader with business targets to meet, who holds the purse strings and often gets to make the final decision or give approval for his subject area. There is also the internal communication professional who acts as a trusted adviser to the leader, say, a leader like Sean. They are both experienced and confident. Third, we have the most important of the people, the employees in our company. From the CEO to frontline staff, they are the people whom we want to be communicating with. Lastly, we have the technology, the newcomer who wants to grab the glory.

The Business Leader

As any good leader knows, they are responsible for making the best decision. The senior business leader holds the budget and approves the internal communication approach. With this immense power, the business leader can decide how critical messages are communicated. Every internal communication professional has an example of how their internal client wanted a video for a project, and insisted on a video, even though from a communication perspective it had no value. For one such situation, I know a very expensive short video was watched 250 times in an organization of approximately 20,000 people, ending up costing a lot of production and promotion money per view. In the end, they didn't even know who specifically had watched it, just that it had been watched.

As a 2023 *Harvard Business Review* article states, "Many executives admit they were never taught how to communicate efficiently or profitably. And many more feel poorly set up to lead in an environment that has radically changed: the in-person workplace."

Many leaders teach themselves how to communicate within their organization because their role requires it to climb the corporate ladder. Communicating effectively at scale brings power, knowledge, and success. So, what if you knew what this looked like? What if you could confidently ask the right questions and satisfy yourself that your internal communication at scale will help to effectively reach your business goals? This matters because AI products that will spit out a strategy are already on the market. Knowing if it is good and meets your organizational needs is up to you.

Communicating at scale within an organization is a business function. Similar to the finance function, leaders need a good understanding of this to be effective. They should also look to the experts who understand how to communicate with different groups of employees within an organization.

Internal Communication Professional

Internal communication professionals trade in influence, knowledge, understanding, engagement, and persuasion. Communication is both a science and an art at the same time. As communication specialists, we are the ones who are often the first to know of organizational success and failure, and will have the responsibility to craft and frame it so that our people understand what is happening. Our role is to push back on senior leaders when their fantasy runs away with them and be the ones they first seek out when our business needs to know something. This, of course, depends on the level of experience and expertise of the organization and its professionals.

Based in the United Kingdom, Rachel Miller is the Founder of All Things IC and focused on upskilling internal communication professionals so they can thrive in their role as effective trusted advisers. Rachel talks about the skills that internal communication professionals need to excel, in her book *Internal Communication Strategy: Design, Develop, and Transform Your Organizational Communication* (2024).

> An internal communicator's attitude (mindset) matters just as much as their competencies and experience (skill set). To be successful as an internal communicator requires working on both. If you have incredible knowledge about the profession, or your organization, but lack the belief or confidence to have difficult conversations with stakeholders or champion employees' voices, it's difficult to operate at a strategic level.
>
> —Rachel Miller

It is the stakeholder management skills that separate internal communication professionals, particularly at the executive adviser level. I often despair when an internal communicator who is starting out in their career is teamed with an opinionated leader and becomes the button pusher or doer without being encouraged or expected to diplomatically challenge decisions or play the crucial role of bringing diverse stakeholders together toward agreement. This is a skill that I focus on supporting others in developing because I see what a huge difference it makes in their ability to be effective at the trusted adviser level. I know there are other practitioners including Rachel who see this the same way. In the future, these consultancy skills are where the value lies in the profession, what leaders should look for when hiring, and where investment for professional development should go.

"We need to create conditions where internal communicators can develop in their existing roles and be treated as the counsel they are," Rachel said.

In some countries, internal communication as a profession is still relatively new. Such professionals can sometimes be relegated to organizing the company party, with little business or strategic purpose other than keeping staff happy or engaged.

In a small organization of 100 people, internal communications may be managed by an HR employee with a communication part to their role, helping the CEO align the troops' understanding of where the company is going and how they can best contribute.

For larger organizations, teams of internal communicators can be scattered throughout or in a central function. They can be the wordsmiths, graphic designers, video teams, ESN community managers, and strategists who collectively help the information flow and align an organization, bringing the organizational culture to life. Sometimes their efforts are coordinated, and occasionally little fiefdoms emerge under ambitious leaders who run their own agendas.

You can't see me, but I am smiling as I think of one of my previous clients who is not only extremely charming and witty but is also a politically ambitious head of information security within a global company. His communication budget is bigger than the central internal communication team's budget, and he has hired his own people to run his own campaigns, how he wants them. Although he gives a big grin and his eyes crinkle at the corners when he says he isn't interested in leadership positioning, I know that the visibility of his position both within and external to the company is important to him, and he is pleased when his topics gain attention. He is a smart leader who knows there is value in communicating effectively at scale, but doesn't always know how it should be best done, nor should he know. This is why he has internal communication experts to help him reach his ambitious project goals.

Over 10 years ago, the rule of thumb was one internal communication titled professional per 1,000 employees. Over the last few years, through my consultancy work and poking my nose into different organizations, I have seen a lower ratio, with at least one person responsible for internal communication in any organization with over 150 employees. Gallagher's State of the Sector 2022/23 research, looking into internal communication practices of more than 2,000 organizations globally, places small companies of 0 to 499 employees as having, on average, just over two dedicated internal communicators. This jumps to nearly five dedicated professionals for large organizations of 1,500 to 5,000 employees and then about 11 for enterprises of over 10,000 employees. This does not account for all HR professionals or other employees who handle internal communication as part of their job. In-house designers working on internal and external projects and the intranet team are also not included in these numbers.

Times when you'd want extra internal communication professionals on hand are when you're communicating across several different cultures and more thought needs to go into cultural and linguistic nuancing or when you have a high-risk, business-critical project.

Colleagues, Employees, and Staff

Whatever your company preference is for the name of people employed in your organization, these people are your target audiences for different communication campaigns.

They could be your call center staff, your bus drivers, your office workers in a specific location, or your new graduates. They could be your engineers or developers in your mar-tech start-up in Berlin or your board of directors.

There is the temptation to talk about employees or staff in a general sense, but this loses the nuances of each group. When communicating at scale, they must be broken down into different groups and cohorts depending on your goal. No two groups of people are the same.

Many of them will be your stakeholders. With change communication projects I often find it hard to separate out the idea of the target audience and stakeholders and think of all of them as stakeholders. You wouldn't be communicating with them unless whatever you wanted to discuss had meaning and an impact on them. These are just my views, and I haven't heard them expressed elsewhere yet.

The Technology Revolution

Technology impacts how we do our jobs and communicate within an organization. It is also a player in our game of people and one of the stars in our story.

We are now going through a technological revolution sped up by the practicalities of remote working, thanks to the pandemic. During lockdowns across the globe between 2020 and 2022, computer-based workers, or "desktop jockeys," were forced to work remotely. As a result, our approach to work has shifted dramatically, and there are no significant variations between countries and types of organizations. Many companies are attempting to bring employees back to the workplace successfully, and others are still working out where they have landed on their hybrid policies. Employees are evaluating what work and workplace flexibility means to them.

Technology is in the middle of this mix of workplace behaviors and expectations. An assortment of platforms and tools have been rapidly implemented, often needing a strategic, holistic channel management approach. Some organizations are still operating in suboptimal technology conditions, for example, relying on faxes to send information reliably or having regular company wide e-mail outages. In contrast, others have sophisticated, digital workspaces with an intranet that customizes the information and tasks for the person, their role, and their location. Back in 2019, at the Digital Employee Experience conference in Sydney, one of my fellow speakers, Christy Punch, from Wells Fargo in South Carolina, United States, gave an impressive insight into their award-winning digital workplace, Teamworks. The workspace supported more than 257,000 team members from 37 countries and territories. Christy's team used microservices architecture as a technical foundation to ensure a great employee experience.

Now, with the latest out-of-the-box mainstream products, digital workspaces are often customized to the role function, location, seniority, and what they subscribe to. Once AI-powered, the personalization and customized content will be able to be truly tailored to the individual level and their preferences. The spread of technology being used is widening, software integration within an organization can also be variable, and more tools are constantly being added to the mix.

We also have technology that allows for more channels. ESNs have quiz functions and are like mini social media channels. We can build mini-metaverses for our staff, and we have several different brands of employee communication apps to choose from to reach remote workers. Marry this with social media and blogs, and we have democratized content distribution with algorithms.

There is also much variance between what types of technology our people are being exposed to outside of an organization, especially now that employees in many organizations are expected to use their own devices for work purposes.

We're living in a world of change, but we're not all advancing equally.

We also have many senior leaders who have always done things a certain way and will need to be guided on the journey. You may personally know some of them. Please think of the executive who doesn't know how to turn on the telepresence in their office or who will only read printed documents. As you present your concepts to them on a video call, you can see them not looking at you or the screen but rather flicking through the color printout their assistant handed them 30 minutes before.

But this book isn't about how to choose and implement technology. It is about internal communication strategy. How to be strategic. How to know if your strategy is any good at a glance. The technology, however, sets the scene for where we're operating right now with organizational communication. Lots of possibilities. No one real solution.

How Will AI Impact Organizational Communication?

It isn't just me; my manager Sean who has been thinking about AI, or the people in the risk department or across the organization working in silos on the same issues. All have similar concerns. There are communication professionals, from marketing experts to freelance graphic designers, who are both fascinated and unsettled by the speed of technology advancements. In early January 2023, more than 6,000 different AI tools for public relations (and communication) professionals were identified by the Chartered Institute of Public Relations (CIPR).

For example, speech recognition for language translation is an obvious AI add-on to any intranet site or employee app. With new products coming out every day, some use aggregating translations of the text from different products to produce the most accurate translation. Microsoft O365 products have had translation functions built in since 2018, and subtitles during video calls (in Teams) are now possible. Automatic language translation into your preferred language opens up the world to new possibilities to communicate quickly in a digital world.

I've spoken with many communication thought leaders globally about how AI will impact our roles, and all agree that the most successful of us in communication roles will need to become the puppet masters of whatever the current AI platforms offer and be able to work with them effectively.

Rubbish in gives rubbish out. Prompt engineering will become a core skill for any communication professional. This is knowing what to ask

GenAI programs to get the results that you want. I can see the more entry-level communication roles transferring from being the drafters of content, to being the prompt engineering experts, needing to consistently identify and share the best prompts, to get the best content out of AI. I can also see that there will be a role for someone who keeps data and input clean and at a quality level. This includes making sure the company style and language guide is correctly loaded and up to date in AI-enabled programs so all users can efficiently produce content that is on-brand and reflecting company tone and content style.

There will also be a role for those working even more closely with the technology team to analyze how communication is being produced and identify production efficiencies. This sounds very high level, but it basically means making sure all of your mar-tech (marketing technical stack) talks to each other and you're only using sensible add-ons, whether it is the right language translation tools for your intranet product or a powerful sentiment analysis tool, to meet the specific communication needs of your organization.

You can't run fast if you don't have the right shoes (and your laces are tied).

Technology and AI are great for data crunching, spotting patterns, ideation, and a number of other things, but in the end, it is up to us mere humans to take responsibility and make the decision around what is good. Is that video good and will it be effective? How does it fit together with the bigger picture and bigger strategic approach to our change campaign? Even more importantly, we'll need to be confident that we're taking the right big-picture approach to reaching whatever communication and business goals we've set.

In September 2023, at the Nordic Business Forum, the previous chief business officer at Google, Mo Gawdat, gave a great analogy that has stuck in my head. He said that when someone throws a ball and you want to catch it (for some reason I have a red, smooth tennis-sized ball in my mind), you should run to where the ball is being thrown, not to where the person is who is throwing the ball. In the same way, we should constantly be looking to what could be possible with AI and technology and use this to help us plan for the future. Focusing on where the ball is right now doesn't make sense as it is moving too fast.

The future of AI is so unknown and so hyped right now that even the best minds cannot predict with confidence when AI will outstrip human intelligence and what this could mean. Mo has laid his bets on pre-2026. We will see.

Questions to Ask to Better Understand Your Internal Communication Environment

- What skills do my internal communication professionals have?
- Can skills and experience gaps be filled through new hires, an external agency or team training?
- Is the internal communication team well connected and working closely with the HR team (sometimes called personnel) and the information technology (IT) team?
- Are there other teams they need to work with to get the results I want?
- How is AI being used and how could it be used to improve how internal communication is done in my organization?

Discussion: Thoughts From the Thought Leaders

I finally met Shel Holtz in person in New York during the IABC World Conference 2022 over the best pastrami on rye I've ever had. Shel has been an organizational communicator for over four decades and is globally respected for his internal communication and digital technology thought leadership. Following my presentation on immersive communication with Andreas Ringsted, Shel's session drilled down, focusing on metaverses. I've seen Shel present many times, and it has always been insightful.

While I was bravely trying to conquer my double towers of pastrami at Ben's Deli—my husband is vegetarian and the main cook, so this was a rare treat for me—Shel and I had a great discussion about what the future brings for internal communication. Shel is a considerate and thoughtful converser, and we talked a lot about the opportunity to use more audio in internal communication. This was in the context of multisensory communication techniques, which I cover in my chapter about immersive communication. More recently, I looped back to Shel for his thoughts on how AI will impact us and the communication profession.

> The time I save using AI enables me to spend more time doing the work that demands human creativity, especially writing. If communication leaders don't figure this out, AI/communication start-ups will eat away at our credibility and work. It's worth remembering that communication leaders woke up to the web when web-focused boutiques began grabbing client work that traditionally went to PR agencies, reaffirming my belief that the communication profession doesn't evolve until it feels enough pain.
>
> For communication leaders to reject AI out of hand is not just short-sighted. It's irresponsible.
>
> —Shel Holtz

When I spoke with internal communication thought leader and friend Mike Klein in early 2023, he agreed with this sentiment. Mike is the kind of person who has his own opinions and is only tempted to agree with something if he actually does. Mike also gets bonus points for inviting us all to Ben's Deli on W 38 Street in New York City, where I met Shel and other great communicators and first fell in love with pastrami on rye.

"The bad news is that AI will take much of the journeyman writing," Mike said from his office in Iceland over our video call in January 2023. "Commoditized work will be hard to find, and there will be a need for specific skills that cannot be commoditized, such as organizational connectivity and influence. Our roles will become the conceivers, fine tuners, positioners, and adapters."

For those of us who work in multilingual environments, we've already seen the huge benefit that AI has brought with language translation, but we still need experts who know if the translation is correct, making sure it reflects the right framing, meaning, and cultural context. This example can be applied more broadly to communication and communication strategy.

If you want to effectively communicate at scale within your organization, you still need to understand what best practice looks like and what will get results.

> ## Key Takeaways
>
> We are going through a technological revolution—AI is changing how we work, including how content is produced. More sophisticated communication tools are available for the workplace, which offers more flexible ways of working, needing more tailored approaches to internal communication.
>
> - Strategic internal communication has been proven to have a huge, positive impact on business results.
> - Internal communication is a profession that requires specific skills and knowledge for the practitioner to be able to act as a trusted adviser and business partner to effectively support leaders and business.
> - Different organizations are moving at different paces on the technology front.
> - Employees have more diverse expectations based on their personal experiences with technology.
> - Because of increasing business and global complexity, effective internal communication is more important now than ever.

CHAPTER 1

Good, Better, Best Strategic Internal Communication

The Technological Revolution Is Here

The perky but somewhat monotone American voice sang the praises of internal communication while corporate images flashed across the screen.

A few months ago, Keith, one of my graphic designer friends in Johannesburg, South Africa, was playing around with making a fully AI-generated video, using different products to generate the script, static images and videos, enhancements, and even an AI-generated voice-over. It was a one-minute video on the benefits of internal communication using only AI tools: he'd used ChatGPT for the script, 11ElevenLabs for speech synthesis of the voice-over, and Mubert for the soundtrack. He experimented with Leonardo Ai for the visuals. However, his prompting produced strange results, so he resorted to Pictory, which collates stock video.

When Keith shared the video on a company morning video call, we were all impressed, at least until we looked closely. The content was very generic and quite boring. It lacked the sharpness of the message, and the content wasn't entirely correct. Keith explained where the GenAI images had gone wrong, like a person's arm blending into a table or a bit of an ear missing. The voice lacked emotion, and the result was far from engaging.

I sensed that our global team of internal communication professionals were both excited at what AI tools could do for us and, at the same time, relieved that we wouldn't be losing our jobs just yet—at the time we felt we could still beat GenAI when it came to defining quality as well as giving something the right edge. But for someone who doesn't know the difference between what is correct and good from a content, engagement, and employee perspective, they might have been happy with the result that Keith achieved in July 2023. Since then, text-to-video generation has continued to develop rapidly with OpenAI producing impressive cinematic showreels. By March 2024, Sora, OpenAI's 60-second video generation product was poised to launch, with unanswered ethical questions and some minor flaws—hands still being problematic. Adobe had also incorporated a powerful and fully functional generative imaging tool that could fill in blank spaces on photos, create an entirely new picture, or fill in the image from prompts. Public scandals had already occurred, such as an Australian politician being depicted in a crop top as the result of the Adobe Photoshop AI expand tool.

We've got to be vigilant as the keepers of quality, what is true and what is right.

Content Is Now Cheap

GenAI, which is the type of AI that produces content, is both the biggest opportunity and threat to so many professions. A June 2023 McKinsey report predicted that 75 percent of the value that GenAI brings will mostly impact roles in customer operations, marketing and sales, software engineering, and research and development. For such a huge impact on the way, many professions are still at the play-with-it stage, while others are furiously implementing and improving, moving rapidly toward a more productive standpoint.

Newsrooms already use different types of AI for lead generation and investigative journalism, content creation and distribution, and engaging with their readers. For example, the BBC newsroom uses AI for social media listening (CrowdTangle 2023), audience engagement and community management (Hearken 2023), easy audio and video conversion to text for editing and sound and visual enhancement (Descript 2023), and natural language generation to write reports and articles based on data sets (Arria 2023). News Corp is also using AI to write headlines among other things.

Organizations are already playing with content generators to draft e-mails and intranet news stories and help with ideation and proofreading. Some companies I work with already have closed generative GenAI systems to prevent employees from putting confidential information into ChatGPT, such as Samsung employees did in April 2023. Samsung engineers accidentally leaked internal source code by uploading it to ChatGPT. Rumor has it that no one was quite sure what happened to the information or where it would turn up on the public platform. The use of ChatGPT was banned in the company following this incident.

Another business is using AI for organizational listening to source all of the company app comments from staff and analyze the sentiment. The tool allows for slicing and dicing of data and multilingual analysis. Once fully functional, it will be a powerful way to identify hot spots and issues in real time that staff are vocal about. It will make feedback on their organizational communication much easier and instantaneous.

For many, company policies are still being developed and refined, as are broader country and regional laws around the use of AI. For example, it wasn't until March 13, 2024, that the European Parliament approved the first Artificial Intelligence Act to help provide safety and compliance with fundamental human rights.

How Do You Know If Your Internal Communication Is Good?

With all the new tools at our fingertips, our new challenge in the age of AI is knowing if what we're looking at is good or not. It is knowing what questions to ask to make it better, or even the best that it possibly can be.

German philosopher, author, and researcher Jürgen Geuter gave a hilarious example from the large language models (LLM) website in his keynote on Communication in the Era of Chatbots at the biggest European communication profession conferences, the Kommunikations Kongress 2023 in Berlin. It was a simple math problem, which makes it easier for us as there is only one right answer.

The prompt asked: Sally (a girl) has three brothers. Each brother has two sisters. How many sisters does Sally have?

We all know the correct answer is one.

ChatGPT 3.5 Turbo (from 2022) answered the problem with the following:

- "Sally has three brothers, and each brother has two sisters. This means that Sally is one of the sisters of each of her brothers. Therefore, Sally has three sisters."

ChatGPT 4 (released 2023) came back with the following answer:

- "Sally has two sisters."

LlaMA 2 SFT v 10 (708 (Meta) replied with the following:

- Sally has three sisters.
- Here's the step-by-step reasoning:
  1. Sally has three brothers.
  2. Each of her brothers has two sisters.
  3. Since there are three brothers, and each brother has two sisters, there are a total of 3 * 2 = 6 sisters.
  4. We know that Sally is one of the sisters.
  5. Therefore, Sally has five sisters in total.

The generated answers may progressively have less sense. Just because the machine produces the content, strategy, or plan with human input doesn't mean that it is good or even correct.

Numerous studies have demonstrated apparent weaknesses in AI reasoning, including the one published in NewsGuard. Around 60 models were tested on basic reasoning, instruction following, and creativity and results were displayed on an LLM Benchmark website. An LLM Benchmark is a standardized software performance test that benchmarks different LLMs such as ChatGPT. Some of the creativity testing examples, based on "writing a product description for a 100 W wireless fast charger for my website," were extremely creative and did not correlate with what was logical, true, or accurate as websites don't need fast chargers. The LLM test request had been absurd; however, the machine hadn't known.

As soon as we add nuanced and complex information to the mix, we need to remember that our judgment and evaluation of what is quality, what is correct, and what will give results, is more valuable than ever.

When I followed up with Jürgen after the conference, he enthusiastically agreed, saying "AI systems are good at producing text that looks somewhat human, by mimicking structural patterns from their training data without any understanding or regard for the actual meaning of the output. They offer all form but no substance."

I did my own checks in October 2023 and found that Sally still had two sisters according to ChatGPT 3.5, but Google's product Bard told me that Sally had one sister. On a side note, Bard was renamed Gemini in February 2024. At this point, I checked in again with Chat GPT 4+, who now confirmed with me that Sally had only one sister.

When talking with Robert, a previous newsroom guru turned investor, at the Australian Embassy over a BBQ democracy sausage with ketchup, he assured me that this was a perfect example of the speed at which the technology is improving. His advice was to ask the prompt at least 10 times to keep training the AI to give the correct answer. Again, the problem is that the human needs to know the correct answer and recognize what good looks like.

When we start to make our communication more complex, where one piece of communication follows on or is related to other messages and initiatives, it becomes even more fraught with danger.

For example, a video or an e-mail usually sits within the communication of a bigger project. The bigger communication project should always be linked to business strategy. Just as a business strategy is usually not just one initiative to get the desired results, a communication strategy has different tactics or initiatives to create your desired impact. It makes sense to combine and consider the bigger picture and fit each communication piece together to result in a more significant impact on your people.

AI agents are on the way that can create complex communication campaigns. They are self-organizing, different AI technologies that work together and are goal completion focused. The idea would be that with the right prompts, the technology could create and execute a campaign producing all of the necessary artwork, videos, intranet news articles, and Viva Engage posts needed. Again, my question would be, how do we know if it will be strategic and effective? A human will need to make that decision.

As a discipline, internal communication adds the most value when it is strategically thought through and executed with purpose. This means being deliberate with the choices you make. From whom you communicate with and in which order to the choice of words and images, all need to be chosen with consideration. Just as a business strategy outlines how an organization will get from the current state to a specific future state, being strategic with internal communication is the same. The approach must be directly linked with business objectives and make sure that our people, leaders, and organization benefit from the money, time, and resources invested in the communication.

As technology has evolved, so have our approaches to communication strategies. At the most basic, we have the broadcast message. Think of this like smoke signals that could be spotted in the sky if the wind isn't blowing too hard. Next, we have the two-way sender–receiver model. A perfect example is an e-mail or snail mail post delivered to your door by a cheery postie.*

In 2006, Facebook was made public to everyone over 13 with an e-mail address. Social media grew, and we shifted to building digital communities. The technology has allowed us to focus more on creating and interacting with communities as a part of our approach to communicating at scale. For example, when I was an intern in 2002, post September 11 in Washington, DC, most of our public relations activity involved media relations or investor relations. We tried to influence what the newspapers, television, and radio journalists would publish to shift public perception of the product, brand, company, or person we represented. Now influencer management is replacing a lot of the media relations work we used to do. This is about working with specific social media content creators to spark discussions and influence within specific communities. These public relations techniques are still maturing as their use expands within organizations.

With the growing use of AI and immersive technology influencing how we think and interact with content, we need to shift our mindset again to build these characteristics into how we communicate at scale within organizations.

With an understanding of strategic internal communication models and knowing which questions to ask, you will quickly be able to spot where something has been overcooked, has gaps, lacks thinking, or in the best case, is going to kick goals. You'll also be able to ask the right questions to find out if what you plan to do will get results.

---

* A postie is Australian slang for the person who delivers your mail to your house. They are usually on a motorbike or a pushbike.

The Value of Internal Communication to Your Business

Why communicate with your people? Why communicate with them at scale? It all comes down to productivity, efficiency, and employee retention.

Good internal communication brings value through the following:

- **Corporate communication:** Helps your people understand where the company is going so they can make the right choices in their daily jobs and reduce confusion.
- **Organizational listening:** Gives you insights that inform the best decisions.
- **Effective change and transformation:** Supports your people through the change process.
- **Streamlining communication:** Combats the information burden weighing down your people.

The value is always linked back to business goals.

Corporate Communication

If your people understand where the company is going, why it exists, and the corporate goals, it is easier for them to make the right decisions to help the company succeed. If you are a good communicator as a leader and well positioned, not only will you be able to play a role in helping your people understand the direction of the company, but they also will be more likely to follow you and give you more slack when things go wrong. If you have a strategy, whether it is your corporate strategy or a substrategy such as culture or corporate responsibility ESG (Environmental, Social, Governance), internal communication is needed to inject life into it. Organizational culture only exists through actions and communication.

Numerous studies have shown that getting strategy communication right is fundamental to boosting employee engagement. This idea was supported by a study conducted by Ipsos Karian and Box for the IoIC in March 2023 that looked at 3,000 employees in the United Kingdom from organizations with at least 500 employees. It showed that with employee engagement comes increased discretionary effort, and greater employee retention, to name a few benefits.

A key part of corporate communication that many people forget is alignment, that is making sure that everyone has the same basic understanding. This is discussed in more detail later, in the chapter on alignment.

Organizational Listening

Information flows in all directions. Being able to hear what your customer-facing staff are experiencing can give vital business knowledge, as can picking up on any friction in different areas of the business. If you can identify a problem quickly, it is easier to address it. If you know something is going well, it is easier to support and scale.

Effective Change and Transformation

Digital transformation, mergers and acquisitions, restructures, new leaders, new products, new business lines, new corporate strategies, and new initiatives, all require our people to go through change. Irrelevant to your preferred change model, the change needs to be communicated with your people. Bad change communication results in confusion, unhappy and disruptive people, and your talent leaving. This is worse than ineffective change, where nothing happens. With bad change communication, there are many risks that are often overlooked by leaders who are not willing to invest, including the risk of reputational damage to your company brand. Everything communicated within your company is usually considered external, so in the same way, please don't presume that what you do within your company isn't also being noticed outside of your company. The negative impacts of reputational damage are many and often a clean-up is costly.

Streamlining Communication

Pumping too much information at people in your organization is counterproductive, distracting, and confusing. It could also negatively impact your employees' understanding of company strategy. Many people think about the time taken to create content as a cost, but they don't take into account the cost on the receiver side. I find it useful to calculate how long it would take an employee to consume and make sense of corporate information sent to them and then multiply it by the average cost of employment per hour and the number of people you're expecting to send it to. Are you ok with this combined cost (production and consumption) to your company? What is the cost of not communicating? Can it be communicated more effectively? This is also a useful way of looking at meetings.

In their 2023 *Harvard Business Review* article on reducing information overload in organizations, Klein, Earl, and Cundick say that conservatively, an employee, including managers, wastes nearly three and a half hours a week dealing with information burden. That makes the information burden a serious eater of time and productivity.

Additionally, an earlier 2021 Gartner research project of 1,000 companies showed that the number of employees who understand and are aligned with company strategy decreased by over half when they felt overloaded. The survey found that 27 percent of employees reported feeling at least somewhat overloaded by information, and 38 percent of the surveyed said they felt they received an excessive volume of communication at their organization. Most of the information was a duplication of information they had already received, and nearly half of the people said the information was irrelevant to their daily work. Thirty-three percent said the information was inconsistent or conflicted with other information.

Having a plan that links what you are communicating and how you are communicating it is essential, and **taking a strategic approach** reduces the information burden on your people. Being strategic coordinates the bigger-picture information experience and ensures that only the people who need to know are informed. Good audience segmentation helps with this, a critical element of a good strategy, as does the right technology that makes this easier.

Admiring an Elegant Strategy

Nothing is more beautiful than a witty line of prose or an elegantly turned strategy. The beauty is in the simplicity of strategy design, clear ideas, and audience-centric focus.

This is where I confess that I get a warm fuzzy feeling when I look at a linen cupboard and see a stack of towels all neatly folded the same way from smallest to largest. An open wardrobe with all tops neatly arranged from light colors, through the color spectrum to black, will also do the trick for me. It is the same feeling I get when I've crafted an elegant internal communication strategy or admire one skillfully created by a fellow professional. There is a challenge in simplicity, from what you include in the plan to what you leave out. Think of the work of a sculptor, a creator of art. What is removed from the marble or block of wood is just as important as what is left behind.

Being strategic with communicating at scale within an organization is like being strategic with business. You'll be surprised at how many elements are similar. It is about working out where you are, where you want to get to, and how you'll get there. The plan lays out the steps. It requires the same rigor, strategic thinking, and stakeholder management skills. The result is thought-out, documented, and can be shared with others for a common understanding. It should always link directly to your business goals.

The reason why we create strategies is to put our thinking down on the proverbial paper. This makes it easier to get agreement when we have a range of people involved. It gives them something tangible to critique. A handy technique I often use with clients who don't exactly know what they want is to draft the final product, such as an e-mail or speech and encourage them to be involved in shaping it. You can tease out and work through the strategic elements through this process to help you get to the answers.

The CEO and cofounder of Airbnb, an online marketplace that connects people wanting to rent their homes with people who want somewhere to stay, used this very same approach when he needed to tell his employees about layoffs following the global lockdown at the height of the Covid-19 pandemic, which brought travel to a standstill. Brian Chesky said that he started with the message that he wanted to send his people and then used this to sense-check the policies they created around how the 25 percent of the workforce who were to be made redundant would be treated.

Not all strategies are equal. This is why, especially with GenAI moving into the realms of strategy development and more content being produced than ever, every leader needs to have the skills to know if the strategy they are looking at is good or not. Is anything missing? Is it overkill and going to waste your budget or will it likely flop because it is simply a blip in the communication landscape within your organization?

For example, an organization ran a campaign targeting deskless staff to download an extra app on their phone. Postcampaign research showed that employees were confused by the messaging and tagline of the campaign because the company already had an app. A new campaign was needed with the right messaging and approach to get the results. This redo cost extra time, money, and confusion among staff. The work needed to be redone.

The person with the budget often differs from the one delivering the strategy. The budget holder, and therefore the power wielder, is also responsible for ensuring the strategy will be effective. With power comes responsibility to do the right thing. The leader with the budget needs to guarantee that money will be well spent and that the communication campaign will likely achieve set business goals. The challenge here is that the person with the power is often not the internal communication expert. But they do need to know what good looks like and what questions to ask the communication expert to make sure that they are spending wisely.

So, What Does a Communication Strategy Look Like?

It can look like whatever it needs to look like. A communication strategy simply needs to answer the question of where are you now, where do you want to get to, how will you get there, and how will you know when you've arrived. You also need to be clear on what resources you need to have to get there and who will do the work, plus how long it is expected to take.

Someone reading your plan for the first time must understand what is being proposed and why. It can be displayed in a presentation format with limited words, or it can be expressed in a lengthy Word document. Having it documented helps when trying to create a shared understanding. It can also help give comfort to leaders that there is a plan.

I need to smile when I remember one of my first internal communication roles and I spotted a colleague, Melanie, cheerfully dumping content into a Word document. I said with confusion, "Oh, that's not in our corporate font?" She said something along the lines of "Don't worry, we're trying to make it look like a consultant did it so management will sign off our plan. It needs to feel hefty and look boring."

Certain characteristics are essential in a good strategy, particularly in this age of AI. The strategy needs to be adaptable so the details can shift and change quickly as the environment around us changes.

A strategy can be as long or as short as it needs to be. It needs to define the following:

- Purpose, problem that you are trying to solve, or opportunity you want to take.
- Background and situation (where you are now).
- Business and communication goals and objectives (where you want to get to).
- Audience and stakeholders (understanding your audience is crucial to any successful strategy).
- Key messages (what you want to communicate with each audience group).
- Risks and mitigation (what could go wrong and how will you prevent this or compensate if it does go wrong).
- Strategy (how you will solve the problem and get from the current state to the future state).
- Tactics (what tools and products, such as an inspiration video or champion network, will be used).
- Implementation plan (what will happen when and who is responsible—sometimes called the action plan, listing all the products that will be created as a part of the campaign).
- Evaluation (how will you know if you've been successful. This should be linked directly with communication goals and objectives).
- Appendix with whatever analysis models are needed, including a SWOT (strength, weakness, opportunity, and threats), RACI (responsible, accountable, consulted, informed), or a stakeholder analysis (stakeholder by importance tier, who influences them, what channels they use and who the key person is responsible for managing communication with them).

I have many different models and variations that I whip out depending on the situation and what we need to look at.

The documents don't need to be long; they just need the necessary information.

One of my most painful experiences was picking up a limping and nearly failed project from the previous project owner that had not one but six separate communication strategies and multipage documents. There was one document for each broad key target group, plus an additional key message booklet. My eyes glazed over from disbelief. I carefully pulled each activity into one plan to determine the timing between the target audiences and activities. I reduced the strategy to two or three pages and combined it with the stakeholder engagement strategy. This was a critical, sizable organizationwide project that had the potential to significantly damage their reputation if something was done out of sync. Confusion about what was supposed to happen when, due to multiple documents would have only increased the risk of reputational disaster. Incidentally, with the slimmed down plan and pretty pitch deck, we quickly got stakeholder support and delivered great results, on time.

Strategies are supposed to be useful; plans are supposed to be easy to follow.

Everyone has their preferences for document length and amount of detail, but this doesn't mean that one should skimp on the thinking that goes behind the strategy for the sake of presenting a high-level, beautiful slide deck.

When Strategy Meets Creative

Strategic thinking needs to be combined with a creative approach, not only in how the business communication problem is tackled but also in how each piece of communication looks. These e-mails, videos, screen savers, digital signage for foyers, or podcast episodes are often called assets or products because they are individual items that need to be created. Each product format has specific characteristics and costs that also need to be considered. For example, a video, even made with AI, costs more time to get right than an intranet news story, which can now be drafted in a matter of minutes once the thinking has been done. A town hall meeting can offer a more nuanced context than a social media post. A town hall meeting is what the name sounds like. A leader or leaders are put in front of employees to present their ideas and answer questions from the audience in an open forum. As it was back in the colonial era of America, when the leader would stand on a balcony and talk to the crowd in the town square, this meeting should be open to everyone who wants to attend.

The messaging, or what you want to communicate with your audience, can be creative and inspiring, as can the visuals that go with it. The colors, image choice, font, and exact words should all be guided by the strategy and created to achieve specific goals.

Being strategic doesn't give us a license to be boring. Far from it! If we want to inspire our target audience, our products, what we say, and how we interact with them need to help them feel inspired. If we are communicating grave news, our tone, creative assets, and products must match this to get the right result with our specific audience.

How Can We Be Better at Strategy?

Practice, practice, practice. Most of my direct reports and other professionals I know have learned how to write a communication strategy similarly—unfortunately, through rote learning, without understanding the principles or elements behind it. They start with a basic understanding of what needs to be included and copy what has been done before using a similar project or audience. I have seen this in consultancy work, where a project is fished out from old files and dusted off. "Ok, let's start with a town hall with the CEO and then launch a video for those who couldn't make it, then make sure we have manager kits so they can cascade." I have also seen it in-house. "Let's do a computer lock screen, an intranet story, and some banner advertising on the intranet pointing to the story," someone would reel off.

Then, as the internal communication professional becomes more experienced, they'll experiment and hopefully see trends and patterns in a specific organization with specific target audiences. They will adjust their approach to what works. For example, one year, for International

Women's Day, an organization I know ran four internal news stories leading up to an event, with a different leader each week. The thinking was that leadership articles are popular; therefore, we'll do four leadership articles, with different leaders. The readership continued to drop as the weeks progressed, which was unusual for leadership articles. Through talking to people in the organization, the project team realized that staff had become disengaged with the topic; this knowledge was incorporated into their learnings, and they took a different approach with subsequent campaigns. A better way is to understand the principles, ask the right questions, and be able to apply them to any situation.

Some CEOs I speak with have their own set play. They do a town hall, e-mail, and then follow up. Sometimes it needs to be more than this, and they need to actively look for opportunities to get feedback and build this into their plan so they can adapt and change from the cookie-cutter approach.

This is why a practical, multilayered strategic approach is important. Think of it as a "layered cake" or a three-level toolbox, where each layer adds depth and complexity to the final campaign. Just as businesses are not built in a day, more effective and sustainable results for internal communication are achieved over time using a multilayered strategy, rather than with a single, isolated approach or by bombarding the audience with the same message in the same way. Again and again.

An elegant strategy needs to efficiently get results without wasting time, money, or resources. It needs to stand up to scrutiny and achieve measurable results. When strategy meets creativity, then you have the sweet spot.

> **Questions to Ask to Make Sure You Understand the Communication Strategy**
>
> - What is the problem?
> - Who does it impact? How many people? Where are they?
> - What is the outcome you want, what do you want them to think, feel, and do?
> - How does it directly support the corporate strategy?

- What is the gap between where you are and where you want to get to?
- How complex is the topic that needs to be communicated? For example, does it involve change and transformation, warranting more complex and nuanced techniques?
- Who are the stakeholders, what are the power plays, and are there any that I need to manage myself?
- What timelines or milestones are there and are they realistic?
- What barriers are there to effective communication at scale?
- What are the risks and how can they be mitigated? Include what happens if no communication or ineffective communication takes place.
- Who can help, and what are their roles?
- What resources are needed? What resources including technology are on hand?

Discussion: The Relationship Between Technology and Internal Communication

As the Head of Digital and Employee Communications at DHL Group, Steffen Henke's team communicates with 600,000 employees worldwide, from pilots to truck drivers, and warehouse crew to office employees. For someone who is at the helm of employee communication at such a large company and with so many years of experience, Steffen is still curious about new communication possibilities, a great conversationalist, and is down to earth. I'd call him a modern leader. He has an impressive background in corporate communication including Head of Executive and Internal Communications at Vodafone in Germany and Head of Communications Region Continental and Northern Europe at the Linde Group.

One of the many things we adamantly agree on is the importance of internal communication in having a very strategic, leadership role. Steffen describes it as "Guiding an employee through the company strategy and where the company is heading," and that this goes hand in hand with the employee experience.

> Steffen said:
> Everyone needs to understand why they are going to work and their role in the big picture, and this has become more complex over the last few years and is the reason why internal communication has become more and more important.

"The story we need to tell has so many chapters in it."

"It's not only top down but also from the ground up, and recent technology development has opened so many opportunities," he said. "Everyone is dealing with a changing technological environment in their daily life."

"The best example is the smartphone," Steffen explained. "Every single one of us has the smartphone as the primary source of information, that is with you all the time."

We talked about how employee communication and company apps compete with the apps and technology and expectations that employees have in their private lives. It's clear that internal communication needs to keep pace with "real life" experience. Steffen is the perfect person to understand the importance of the smartphone following their multiaward-winning digital workspace rollout that incorporates an employee app.

Steffen mused:

> Companies can be boring when they do internal communication and I mean that's one of the challenges. You are on the same platform with all of those other fun, engaging apps on a smartphone. If you continue to communicate as you used to communicate, you won't get that reach you want to achieve.

For me, with 80 percent of the global workforce being frontline staff, AI will certainly have an impact on them, but research shows that the impact will be greater on desk-bound staff. What has the most impact from a communication perspective on the 2.7 billion frontline workers globally as estimated by Gartner or the 2 billion that Microsoft puts it at, is digital communication enabled through employee-owned or company-issued smartphones.

"Let's talk about this other game-changer, AI," Steffen said.

I am sure it will have a huge effect on the topic of language, enabling us in internal communication to reach everyone around the world in their local language. Secondly, it will affect the way we organize our work leading to a transformation of our processes and areas we put our resources to.

But, Steffen also admits that we are still at the very beginning of this journey, where surprises are not excluded.

With all the change technology brings, we need to ensure that our strategy approach is contemporary. Smart. And that it puts us in the right mindset for the future.

Scan to listen

IABC EMENA podcast. "Steffen Henke and Andreas Ringsted on the relationship between technology and internal communication," July 18, 2022. https://on.soundcloud.com/H8Xth

Key Takeaways

Yes, AI and other technologies will impact the way we communicate at scale in organizations. But we still need to know what good looks like. Leaders can benefit from understanding the need for internal communication to be strategic and knowing what a good strategy looks like to help them use budgets, time, and resources wisely.

- Effective communication at scale can help your people understand where you're going, give you insights into your business, support your people through change, and prevent them from being bombarded by confusing or irrelevant information.

- The result is improved productivity, efficiency, and employee retention, with several follow-on benefits, including improved customer experience.
- Internal communication needs to be thought out and strategic in the same way that business strategy exists to help a business get from where it currently is to a future, desired state.
- Business leaders need to understand what a good internal communication strategy looks like and be able to ask the right questions so they can be confident that time, money, and resources will be well spent in getting results for the company.

CHAPTER 2

Content Is King, Strategy Is Queen

Past Ways of Thinking Won't Always Work in the New World

It was so exciting to work on my first virtual reality (VR) project. I had just secured a freelance contract with a consultancy, and things happened fast. I signed my contract overnight before starting the next day, jumping straight into being fully briefed on my first project. Three days later, I delivered a content concept for a new digital, three-dimensional (3D) corporate environment to the client, one of the leading global package transport companies. I felt inspired and couldn't wait to get started.

I had been dropped into the deep end part way through the project. The aim was to engage their people with their corporate strategy, which had been explained to staff as floors and rooms in a house. I freely admit that corporate strategy isn't the most engaging of topics. There is a tendency for it to be dry as dust, intangible, and filled with corporate speak. In the case of this project, my role was to transform a corporate strategy into a play space house that was both interesting and meaningful for the people who worked there. Fortunately, not only was my creative partner, Farzaana Parker a top designer and simply a lovely person to work with, but I also had great stakeholders on the client side, who brought an understanding of strategy, learning and development, and internal communication to the project.

I've done a lot of work as an internal communication professional on intranets and websites. My first project was earlier than 2006— pre-Facebook, and I felt comfortable creating website content and working with designers on the structure. My HTML wasn't too bad, having learned it back in the day, working for one of Australia's top four banks. How hard could designing and creating content for a 3D space be?

Luckily, many foundational things of good communication strategy are transferable between projects. But, over the coming weeks, I needed to rethink how I approached creating the right content for our new 3D space. The layout of the space had already been loosely decided on. We had taken inspiration from real-life spartan office spaces and client warehouse pictures to guide the look and feel.

The 3D characters in the space were designed to act as guides and were modeled on existing characters related to the corporate strategy. There were elevators to take you to the different floors, and each space had a slightly different look and feel to match its purpose. With its clear red and yellow palette, we certainly challenged the branding team with the shadows and lights from a 3D render. But we worked together, and the team took it in their stride.

My favorite space was the conservatorium at the top, with a telescope and a view of the stars when you looked up at the roof. We deliberately kept this space uncluttered. It had a modern inspirational feeling as it housed the strategy vision, mission, and purpose.

I also noticed for the first time that my young boys were interested in what I was doing for work. We'd had weeks of homeschooling due to the Covid-19 pandemic lockdowns in Berlin, and as a treat, they were allowed to sit on my lap at my computer and navigate through the VR space I was working on. At the time they couldn't read, but they could certainly see the bright colors. They were curious and puzzled about my work. To them, it looked like I was playing a Minecraft computer game instead of working. It looked exciting and engaging, and they wanted to play too.

Calling this a light bulb moment seems so 1873, yet nothing better describes that off/on suspension of time when confusion makes sense. I was applying my current thinking of flat, layered two-dimensional (2D) websites onto a whole new dimension. It didn't work.

My eyes were opened to the possible new layers of strategic communication. It was as if my strategic toolbox had suddenly, like in a Harry Potter film, grown to another level. I could see the foundational layer, the networking and community level, and now an additional level that I call immersive communication, which pulls together different techniques to create a new approach. I was able to ideate with Andreas Ringsted, who had been the project sponsor, to form a clear model for this immersive communication.

The DHL Virtual Strategy House won the Digital Communication Awards 2021 for Best Internal Communication. The Quadriga University of Applied Sciences launched the Digital Communication Awards in 2011 as a competition in online communication on both a practical and academic level. An expert jury formed by leading practitioners and academics reviewed outstanding online projects and campaigns. The project lead on the DHL side, Anne Schwartz, Andreas, and I enjoyed showcasing this innovative project at several global conferences.

Let me explain my insights.

Adding Another Layer

Technology evolves, ways of working fueled by the Covid-19 pandemic have evolved, and so should our approach to internal communication. The models that I see most strategists around me using are based on upgrades of the traditional sender–receiver model that is now at least 60 years old.

We don't need to throw away the old models. We can build on them to give us more flexibility. We need to add another layer to our communication strategy.

I smiled when listening to an IoIC podcast on the Future of Internal Communication with guest Seth Godin, a marketing and entrepreneur thought leader. The cohost, Dominic Walters, made the quip that many people would need to retire before we get rid of e-mail, and I thought how true this is. Our communication preferences in the workforce span five generations of workers, from those who still print their e-mails to read them, to others who do most of their business in short message chats.

What isn't working is applying old models to all situations.

The employee communication landscape within many organizations is cluttered with different business areas, from the physical safety team to the new graduate recruitment program, and even the culture team trying to broadcast their messages to all employees through internal news articles or e-mails.

When talking about the number of messages, Seth Godin said "It's not noisy, it's crowded." He said, "It is only noisy when we talk at people, and unfortunately, internal communications has been used as a cudgel by the people running organizations forcing people in internal communication to blast out messages that people don't want to hear."

The solution is not to create more content. It is about being strategically more brilliant.

We need to add another layer to our strategy toolbox that includes techniques that these new technologies can offer. We need to upgrade from the small carry container to a multilevel toolkit that allows us to create the best strategy, clicking the right tactics together for our audience.

Why We Need to Think Differently

Technology has shaped the way we communicate and our expectations around communication. Not only have our norms shifted about health issues such as smoking at the table in a restaurant or our need to be more aware of diversity, inclusion, and equity sensitivities, but technology has also shifted how we communicate with each other. What channels we use, what we say, how we say it.

This new approach to internal communication doesn't require cutting-edge technology such as VR metaverses, augmented reality apps on our phones, or even holograms to succeed. However, by adopting this mindset now, you'll be ready for future advancements in commercially available technology.

Content Is King, but Strategy Is Queen

In 1996, Bill Gates, cofounder of Microsoft, coined the phrase "content is king." It was the title of the essay he wrote published on his company's website about what he thought the intranet would enable.

"Content is where I expect much of the real money will be made on the Internet, just as it was in broadcasting," he wrote.

If content is king, then strategy is queen. Time has moved on from the birth of the Internet. In the age of AI, being strategic will give you so many more moves and enable you to win the game. Like a game of chess, with content only, winning is possible, but so much harder.

Now we need a new three-layer approach to communication strategy. It builds on the old strategy that has evolved to more modern social media-inspired strategic methods and finally adds a new layer that will give us flexibility for the future. This is immersive communication. It is based on learnings from immersive technology. However, it does not necessarily need the technology. It is a mindset—a way of thinking.

When I've spoken at conferences about immersive communication over the last few years, I've had to include fun examples of immersive technology because this is what people want to see and what they sign up to the session for. It is more tangible. The audience loves a good case study; and the metaverse or holograms seem futuristic and exciting.

Unfortunately, it has meant that sometimes audience members aren't receptive to the concepts. They think, "Hey, my organization will never get us all VR headsets," and they have trouble applying the learnings to what they do have. They don't see that their learning and development team has already started using some of the concepts or that other thought leaders are promoting elements of immersive communication.

A little reminder here: 2023 was the year that AI hijacked the technology conversation. Other technologies such as immersive technology, which was the hype of 2021, have fallen out of favor. This is to be expected when looking at the Gartner Hype Cycle for Emerging Tech, a visual representation of expectation on the vertical axis and time on the horizontal axis, taking a specific type of technology through the phases of Innovation Trigger, Peak of Inflated Expectation, Trough of Disillusionment, Slope of Enlightenment and lastly, the Plateau of Productivity. In 2022, Gartner predicted that immersive technology, involving the metaverse, will become more affordable and mainstream in the workplace within the next decade. In their diagram Evolution Spectrum for the Metaverse, Gartner estimated that most people will be accessing an advanced metaverse in 2028. For example, the smartphone, which has been helpful for employee communication apps over the past years, has reached the point, particularly with frontline staff, where in some companies, all staff have been issued smartphones and one can consider smartphones affordable and commonplace for business communication.

I have brought it together into a simple structure for you so you can take it and apply what is relevant to whichever communication strategy you are working on. It means that when you have new technology finally available to you for organizational communication, you'll already be operating with the right mindset.

So, let's break it down into three layers for a closer look and add on leadership communication and strategic alignment. We will then cover what to select and when.

Foundation: Dialogue-Based Communication

More formally known as the Sender, Message, Channel, Receiver (SMCR) model, this is one of the most basic and classic communication theories. In 1960, David Berlo first published this model in his book *The Process of Communication*. In its most basic form, this happens when a person sends another person a message. In my old textbooks, there was always a little broadcast tower icon with a line going to an aerial receiver. For a more modern visualization, think of an e-mail. It is linear. From one sender to another's inbox. The writer's skills and intentions can shape the message. The receiver's state of mind, abilities, and other factors influence how they interpret the message.

Later iterations of the model added a feedback loop and shifted the concept from one-directional to focusing on dialogue. This was discussed a few years later by Lee Thayer in 1968 in his book *Communication and Communication Systems in Organization, Management, and Interpersonal Relations*, where the sender and receiver have repeated transmissions in both directions. The concept has been applied to mass communication and is still evident in most standard communication strategies. Words you will see in these communication plans are "cascade," "all-staff e-mail," or "feedback survey."

From a digital communication perspective, it is very easy to use these techniques as the technology to send and receive instantaneously is widely available. The first text message was sent in 1992, and the World Wide Web was made available to all in 1993.

Network: Multidirectional Communicating Communities

With the boom of social media post-Facebook launch in 2007, companies started to play with enterprise social networks such as Viva Engage,

Facebook for Workplace, and Slack. The multidirectional communication theory was developed and considered essential to using social media for communication. For example, this theory was discussed by Rosemary Thackeray and Brad Neiger in 2009 in their paper *A Multidirectional Communication Model: Implications for Social Marketing Practice*. At this point, the concept of having a network approach to internal communication strategies started to take off, and there was a lot more use of champion networks. This term refers to an interest network engaged within an organization to help spread the word about a given topic. Typical networks include diversity champion networks and change networks. For example, people in the individual groups will meet regularly and be chaired by someone from an HR team. PreCovid-19, they were often site-based, and postCovid-19 you will find most are online as people have become more comfortable with virtual networks. They will have key topics that they are supposed to engage with brought to their attention through the organization networks, and, of course, there are newsletters (e-mails) sent to the group regularly to keep them informed.

Alongside communities in the enterprise social networks, the idea is to "break down silos" and use the "influencer network" to help spread the message. Well-thought-out communities and networks can effectively engage with corporate topics and actively engage the people around them.

Immersive: Audience-Centric Communication

Immersive communication occurs when you put the audience in the center of the experience. You immerse them. You reduce the friction between the messages you want to convey and the conscious processing of the information. It is a multisensory experience that is fluid and puts the control in the hands of your audience for them to choose how they interact with your messages and content, both in terms of order and the type of content. Some of these concepts, such as gamification in campaigns, are not new. Focusing on the audience is not new. Giving them a choice, making the communication nonlinear, is new.

The quickest way to think of these concepts in action is to consider a modern science museum. Anyone who has taken kids to one will know that they start looking at whatever grabs their attention. Most exhibits are grouped in themes with play elements. For example, at Scienceworks in Melbourne, Australia, you can make your own customized car of the future on touch screens, seeing how different materials and feature choices change the sustainability rating. You can take digital snapshots of your car and e-mail them to yourself or a friend. To make the final car, you need to swirl your finger on the touchpad. Your custom car is digitally created in a big swirling ball with whooshing sounds and then projected for all to see on a huge screen filled with the other showroom cars created by others next to you. Multiple car-creation touchscreens are next to each other, so it becomes a shared creative experience with a view of the large showroom screen. Next to this is a display of miniature model vehicles through the ages, and an interactive miniature ecofarm, which extends the sustainability concept. The understanding and "stickiness" of the messaging is so much more effective than if posters had been stuck on a wall.

Immersive communication is where we need to focus to be effective in more complex internal communication strategies.

Leadership Communication

Leadership communication is the cornerstone of successful leadership. It enables leaders to guide, inspire, and engage their teams, leading to better collaboration, productivity, and overall organizational success. Effective leadership communication is essential for change and transformation projects but must be wielded carefully and skillfully to get the desired results. It is also a powerful tool if you want to position yourself for advancement or internal politics. By internal politics, I mean the positioning and shifting moves toward alliances and power that help people get work done the way they want it done.

There are two parts to leadership communication. The first one encompasses interpersonal skills, personal branding, and personal style to achieve your own end; and the second part is a leader's role in communicating at scale to support the success of a communication and change campaign. This is different from external marketing, where the organization's leaders have more of a clear role linked to the business and financials with their personal brand rather than to the product. Exceptions are, of course, for celebrity leaders such as Elon Musk and Jeff Bezos. I'm not sure why these exceptions exist, but I'm guessing it is because they are financially successful, which is what business is about.

If you want to communicate effectively at scale in an organization, you need to understand the different layers in your communication toolbox and how leadership communication operates at all levels. As a leader, it is not about being the voice for everything, but rather being selective in what you are visible with and how you give your voice to an initiative.

Alignment and Stakeholder Management

Corporate strategy and stakeholder alignment is the second part of my model, which I would argue is more crucial to internal communication than other areas of communication such as business-to-consumer (B2C) marketing.

This alignment occurs when everyone understands what they need to do and is motivated to do it.

Aligning an enterprise's purpose, business strategy, organizational capacity, resource architecture, and management systems is one way to look at the topic, which is the perspective Jonathan Trevor and Barry Varcoe give in their 2017 *Harvard Business Review* article. From a communication perspective, it doesn't matter how well aligned these components are, unless the people in the organization at multiple levels understand the business strategy and their role in supporting it, "activity will be mistaken for progress."

This alignment of critical elements is about empowering the people in your organization to understand enough to make sound and informed decisions. It is also about having or garnering support for your projects so that people want them to succeed.

In an organization, there is often significant overlap between target audiences and stakeholder groups, just in the same way that employees can also be potential customers. I am a big advocate for stakeholder engagement and communication both being included in one plan. This makes communicating with the right people in the correct order simpler.

MULTILAYERED INTERNAL COMMUNICATION MODEL

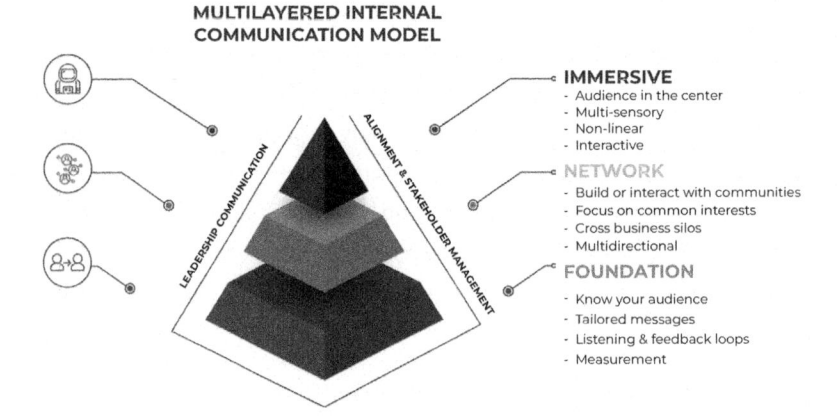

○ **IMMERSIVE**
- Audience in the center
- Multi-sensory
- Non-linear
- Interactive

○ **NETWORK**
- Build or interact with communities
- Focus on common interests
- Cross business silos
- Multidirectional

○ **FOUNDATION**
- Know your audience
- Tailored messages
- Listening & feedback loops
- Measurement

My multilayered internal communication model is ideal for big-picture thinking and discussions, and a great way to visualize and categorize the different elements, tools, and tactics that fit together as a part of an internal communication strategy.

More Tools in the Toolbox

With three neat and orderly levels in our communication toolbox, finding the right tool for the job is easier than ever. Leadership communication and alignment with stakeholder management are two key components that run throughout all the layers, holding everything together.

Understanding the concepts makes it easier for you to substitute different formats or channels to get similar outcomes. For example, if you don't have a preference for particular organizational communication channel and know what you want to achieve, you can find multiple ways to get the same result. Think of it like being confident but not perfect in the kitchen. If you have a basic idea of what different ingredients do, it is easier to substitute to get similar results or to enhance a recipe you have been given to your taste. For example, if my boys and I are making muffins and I've run out of butter I can substitute olive oil and maybe a dash of yogurt, as long as there's enough vanilla or other flavors to cover the missing buttery taste.

By understanding my multilayered communication model you'll be able to:

- More easily achieve your communication goals: Strategy is a roadmap for achieving specific goals. Understanding strategy

allows individuals and organizations to identify the most efficient and effective ways to achieve their objectives.
- Efficiently use resources: An effective internal communication strategy can reduce excessive communication and save employees from information overload.
- Enable adaptation and enhanced decision making: I recommend quickly reviewing standard plans weekly and asking yourself if they still make sense.
- Facilitate innovation: Through experimenting with the new variety of tools in your toolbox, such as using audio, you'll be able to encourage innovative campaigns.

Understanding how effective communication at scale works and my multilayer model is more important than ever. We have increasing complexity of our workforces and change within our world impacting businesses. Of particular concern is the speed at which technology, and specifically AI, is advancing.

So What Does a Communication Strategy Look Like?

A simple project needs a simple communication solution. A more complex and extended project will need more sophistication. There is a sliding scale of sophistication from the simple provision of information, such as an e-mail to staff on level 5 that the toilets are out of order, to a more nuanced communication and change campaign to encourage staff to return to the office after lockdown.

Plans are perfect only in the moment they are created.

As we all know, circumstances change. New stakeholders enter the mix, the environment shifts, something breaks, and new information comes to light. This is why communication strategies need to be regularly reviewed to make sure what is planned matches the reality of the moment. For me, this is weekly when in the midst of a regular campaign. During a crisis, it could be daily or hourly. Constant and consistent organizational listening is essential. The continuous pull of data from many sources, both qualitative and quantitative needs to be combined with actually asking people. The communication team needs to adjust the plan using their knowledge and judgment of what is needed. These changes should be clearly communicated by your internal communication professional to you and the rest of the project stakeholders.

A strategy that has been written lays dormant until it is implemented. This is when it is brought to life for all to experience. A strategy that is never implemented and evaluated is just an idea-generation exercise. The impact of implementation and learning from the evaluation are never able to exist. Without implementation, you cannot reach your business goals, and this is ultimately the purpose of internal communication.

Questions to Ask to Understand What Kind of Internal Communication Strategy Might Be Needed

- How complex is the problem we're trying to solve?
- How much change or transformation are we asking our people to undergo?
- How many people will be impacted? Who are they? Where are they?
- What is the business impact if this doesn't go ahead successfully?
- How much time, money, and resources am I willing to invest (or support being invested by the company) to get a result?
- How urgent is this problem and is there a deadline?
- Is the outcome I want realistic given what I know?

At this point in time, questions about technology including AI are only relevant if it is related to a digital transformation project or a smaller technology-related internal communication campaign. Ideally, technology shouldn't influence the choice of communication strategy used. It should only enable the tactics and techniques.

Case Study: Creating Organizational Culture, Not Clutter

It is so tempting to create more content. Keep pushing the same message out again and again.

Culture is tricky because it should be reflected in everything you see, read, do, and experience within an organization. As we've discussed, strategy is essential. A culture strategy is vital for an organization as it articulates how they see their culture and what goals and behaviors an organization values.

A culture strategy document can also be very dull, no matter how pretty your designers make the document. Even more challenging is when your culture strategy needs to be reviewed after a few years—and shock, horror—management decides it is just fine. A few bits and bobs need to be added. That's all. There goes your big bang launch. "We have a new culture strategy, which is the same as before, just a bit longer."

This happened to me when working with one of Australia's largest government departments on how to bring their updated culture strategy to life. It is easy enough to frame the message and launch the document, but what then? How do you engage staff with the new additions?

The strategy had five key cultural traits, each with several descriptors beneath them. Then multiple new behaviors went with each trait. It would have been easy for me to say, right, we'll roll out the behaviors for each trait and describe them through a news story, one each week. Hey, let's feature a leader or staff member. That's a five-week campaign. But it didn't feel right. It was time to ideate with others and bounce ideas.

I like to have time put aside each week for the team to pursue collective problem-solving. It is a way of sharing information and an excellent way to foster psychological safety. I am collaborative, and my best ideas usually come when someone has said something and sparked an idea in me that I can then take away and think about.

Through trying to explain the cultural traits, their descriptors, and the new behaviors in our ideation session, I got myself and my team thoroughly confused. There was too much information that needed to be conveyed. Listening to myself talk, I realized that I was proposing the creation of content for the sake of content, resulting in more noise for our people.

I'm not sure if it was on my run into work the next day or if I woke up in the night, but I realized that we had to look at the bigger picture, and there were opportunities that I was missing to make it interactive or link it with other areas of culture. All we wanted to do was to help staff recognize the right behaviors. Luckily, we had a reward and recognition program linked to our performance portal to celebrate the right behaviors. We had a badge system where you could award other staff members badges that would sit at the end of their performance report with a few heartwarming "thank you" comments. The badges were small, colored icons with a range of choices of badges.

It took me five minutes to convince the head of the culture team to let me get badges for each of the five traits created and uploaded into the system. It took me less than two weeks for different teams across the organization to get the artwork made, uploaded, and tested, plus the news team briefed.

The news team applied the badges to the end of existing news stories—ones that would be published anyway, highlighting which cultural traits (and behaviors) had been showcased in the story. They also included a call to action for staff to award a badge to someone else they had seen demonstrating the same behavior. This encouraged recognition of the desired behaviors and peer-to-peer sharing in a meaningful way. We also ran a light advertising campaign on foyer screens and our intranet to support the initiative.

This is an example of applying the different levels within our new, expanded toolbox. The sender and receiver model was used with the news articles and feedback mechanism. Then Viva Engage was incorporated to give a touch of cross-organizational collaboration and conversation within specific groups such as the Employee Engagement Community. The interactivity element in the strategy was created by encouraging staff to award each other badges. It was also nonlinear, as no particular badge came first, and there were no rules around how many badges needed to be displayed weekly on the news articles or how many badges people could award each other.

Over half of the articles with a badge had a higher than average readership, and combined with the internal advertising style campaign, we were confident that there was enough visibility. What I loved the most was that data showed an increase in the issuing of badges, and more importantly, a few hundred of the new culture ones were issued in the first months. This shows that the number of new badges didn't cannibalize (reduce the number of) the existing ones, people were more actively rewarding badges rather than just switching types of badges. Interestingly, the actual cultural trait badges issued by staff to each other didn't correlate with the ones promoted in intranet news stories for that week. Instead, it prompted people to take action and send the appropriate one to each other when they saw the right behaviors. The badge search term became the most searched-for word on the intranet.

Because we weren't creating new content, we could run this for a few months, certainly beyond the short advertising campaign. And, we continued to see results.

Key Takeaways

Change is business as usual. My simple model for multilayered internal communication helps to quickly identify the complexity needed for an internal communication campaign and also see what could be missing from an existing strategy.

- Adding layers to communication campaigns will give you better results and a more dynamic suite of tools to craft the right strategy.
- Community and networking techniques can be built on top of the foundation.
- Immersive communication requires more persuasive techniques and is good for more complex campaigns with more people and budgets involved.
- Leadership communication, stakeholder engagement, and alignment run throughout.
- You need to be prepared with the right mindset for when the right technology is available for use.

CHAPTER 3

Foundation: The Basics You Can't Miss

A Conversation Is a Dialogue, Not a Broadcast Message

I explained the sender–receiver model to a dear friend last night who was trying to have a conversation with her son, but it wasn't working.

Sandra's grown son was having a tough time finding a job. She'd sent him a lengthy e-mail—firstly, e-mails should never be too long and never be swamped with multiple question marks and exclamation marks, or start with "Do you need a therapist." The e-mail was a few pages long, a generous scroll down to the end. Anyway, surprisingly, or not, she hadn't had a response from him for nearly a week and wanted to e-mail him more information. I took a calming breath and explained.

At its simplest, the sender–receiver model is like two people throwing a ball to each other. What is supposed to happen is that one person throws, the other catches, and then throws it back. But so many things can go wrong.

The receiver has to be ready to catch the ball (and not out to lunch), then they actually need to catch it. Understand it. Then, they need to be able to lob the ball back.

Standing there with a crate of balls, rapidly lobbing them at someone, is also not a good idea unless it is tennis. This is what she was planning on doing. It is also what many internal communication professionals are tempted to do to their audiences. It is what I worry about with the ease of content production. It is what I train many of my team to avoid doing and push back on their internal clients wanting to bombard staff with the same messages in the same channels in the same way, without getting feedback.

As the sender, after throwing the ball, you also need to be ready to catch anything coming back—this is what organizational listening is about. And, if you ever play ball with my boys, you can be sure that something else, and not a ball, will likely come flying back.

The best way to play ball is to have a win–win situation.

On a side note, Sandra is a retired therapist who has studied counseling, family, and art therapy. Her suggestion to her grown son to seek a therapist was well-meaning, with the best of intentions and a warm heart. It shows that all messages are open to interpretation, and context is important.

When we discussed this in detail, Sandra emphasized that her generation was of the letter-writing sort, where long-distance phone calls had been prohibitively expensive. Long, posted letters were the only way to communicate in detail. This is a timely reminder that we currently have five generations in the workforce, all with different communication preferences. Cultures, countries, languages, and even specific cities can shift the meanings of messages and even the rules of the game. Technology has moved so fast, giving more options for communication and linking people from across the globe digitally, each coming to the table with different cultural backgrounds. The world has changed so fast. The workforce has become so much more complex. We need to make even more of an effort to understand the people who we are communicating with.

The Sender–Receiver, a Foundational Model

This is one of the core communication theory models and one I remember learning at RMIT University when I did my postgraduate back in 2002. Attributed to David Berlo, who described it in *The Process of Communication*, published in 1960, it has four elements: source, message, channel, and receiver.

Berlo's model has had many additions and tweaks over time, and technology has evolved since then. At its essence, it is still a foundational concept for people who want to understand communication.

It helps to visualize the model as a checklist to make sure all the key elements are present in a communication strategy. Who is throwing the ball? Who should receive the ball? Are they ready to catch it? Is there a way for them to return the throw? What does the game involve, and how are you keeping score? How are you making sure that you are being inclusive?

This is a dialogue model. You may read about one-directional communication or two-way communication. What we want now is a conversation that progresses over time. Many leaders find it helpful to think about how they are creating a dialogue with their colleagues.

Listen to Matt Walsh, talk about leadership communication, and focus on having a dialogue with your people.

Scan to listen

Monique Zytnik podcast. "Matt Walsh on CEO communication," 2024.
https://soundcloud.com/monique-zytnik/ceo-communication-matt-walsh

Why Is This Important?

If we apply this very transactional concept to the current era, there are still basics that leaders and communication professionals often miss. They are as follows:

- **Understanding your audience**: Are they out to lunch? Do they have the skills and technology to catch your message? Is something else distracting them?
- **Getting your stakeholders on board:** Are they ready to help play the game? Are there clear rules (frameworks) to play within?
- **Organizational listening:** Are you actively listening to what people are saying?
- **Streamlining the communication experience**: Are there too many balls or objects flying through the air simultaneously?
- **Measurement:** What is being thrown? How often is it caught? What happens long term as a result of the whole exercise, and so on?

- **Risk mitigation:** Are you preparing for what could go wrong?
- **Accessibility:** Are your communications inclusive?

Let's go into more depth with each. We'll then cover what this looks like in the strategy. The details are often listed in the communication implementation plan, sometimes called the action plan.

Understanding Your Audience

Be curious. There are so many ways you can slice and dice your audience in an organization. You need to understand the different audience groups to communicate with them at the right time, in the right way, and with the right context to achieve your goals. Sometimes you can be lucky, and someone's done a research report; or perhaps your HR team have useful workforce data. What many people forget is that much has changed since our more experienced people started in the workforce. Posting letters as the preferred method of long-form communication is still within memory. Fax machines were once the latest technology, and typing with your thumbs on a presmartphone, such as a Blackberry, numeric keypad once had the novelty of a new toy.

What seems like many years ago, in 2017, a friend who was in a central internal communication team spent a week each month editing and compiling a PDF newsletter for a team in the organization. I knew this was an annoying but regular part of his job. At some point, he stopped complaining. When I asked him how it was going, he confessed that the internal communication team had discovered that there were only 140 people in the target audience team, which meant that if everyone had read the newsletter, it cost him at least 17 minutes of his time per recipient to produce the newsletter. This did not include the time spent by the different people submitting, reviewing, and approving the content, nor the time spent by employees reading it. I use the word cost here because, in any business or organization where employees are paid, time is money. But, because of the way it was distributed, they didn't even know how many people read it. Someone could have called every single employee and given them a quick summary of the news in the same amount of time. Interestingly, the reason why the newsletter had been a PDF instead of a web page, which would offer more detailed readership data, was because the most senior person in the team liked to read it on their iPad tablet and the technology that was being used for the intranet didn't give a good user experience on mobile devices. Only the senior managers had tablets, so this only affected 10 out of the 170, should they have chosen to read it on a mobile device. Once the communication team in charge realized this, they changed the situation as fast as they could. My friend was glad to be able to spend his time on higher value tasks.

If you have a budget and a pain point, an internal communication audit is well worth it to understand your audience and their needs. It can uncover content needs—for example, when doing an audit for a global consumable company, a sales representative shared how they sometimes learned about their company's new product from their own customers. It was humiliating for both the sales representative and the company. There was no up-to-date product information on the company intranet, and the product development team had gone straight to public social media to share product updates. This meant that company sales representatives, who were supposed to be the experts in what products a company sells, were often caught unaware of what products were available to customers. This had a considerable impact not only on the employee experience but also on the customer experience as well.

Frontline staff, those who are not desk bound and could be delivery people, doctors, teachers, or supermarket shelve stackers, are also a fascinating set of internal audiences. With 80 percent of the global workforce considered frontline and technology evolving so that most people have a smartphone, many app solutions are now available for organizations wanting to connect, align, and communicate better with their employees. We need to understand employees and their pain points and take advantage of the new insights that digitalization offers, and this is the job of your internal communication team.

If time isn't taken to understand the audience, you can find yourself in very embarrassing or potentially explosive situations. One head of division puzzled aloud to his business manager that he had been authentic, but the warehouse staff hadn't been interested in his stories about his kids and his dog. Apparently, they had been more interested in getting something done about the machinery that hadn't yet arrived, which had been holding up their production. This example goes to show how out of touch the head of the division was with his workers. And, in my opinion, it would have been his responsibility to prompt his direct team to brief him on his warehouse people before the site visit.

At the start of my career, a senior leader once advised me never to go into a meeting where I was hoping to influence, without knowing the views of everyone else there. This advice equally applies to senior leaders on their floor walks or site visits, and many ask their communication team to give them a quick brief and some talking points relevant to the specific people they will be meeting. It is the same tactic that politicians use, and for a good reason.

Another great example was given to me by an internal communication practitioner who personifies the idea of a trusted adviser to CEOs. Fiona Benson, with her warm personality and forthright conversation has no qualms about digging around to get to the source of business problems so she can see how best practice internal communication can help.

In many organizations, an ongoing problem is leave. Staff leave balances are too high, creating a significant liability on the balance sheet. It becomes a simple accounting exercise to reduce costs by the end of the financial year by getting staff to take the leave—unless you work in an organization where you lose unused leave by a certain date, or you have unlimited leave (that no one seems to take). In the case of accruing annual leave, it would be easy to run a companywide campaign to get people to take leave. If you're working in a bank, some of the most significant areas of accumulated leave are in customer-facing areas such as bank branches and in call centers with staffing level constraints and rosters that need to balance coverage and expertise across shifts. It makes no sense to harass staff to take leave they cannot take.

"It annoys people when they feel like you're not listening and you don't understand their situation," explained Fiona. In this case, she ran targeted campaigns where hot spots were identified and they knew that staff were able to take the leave.

A good exercise for making sure that you and your communication team understand your internal audiences is to create personas. This exercise forces you to define the typical person in an audience group by creating a person to represent the group. Drill down to what motivates them, what environments they work in, and what their typical workday looks like. Research and ideally field studies should inform this. Conducting field studies allows you to meet with and get to understand your different target audience groups in a structured way. In the next chapter, we talk more about personas, which are often used in marketing and design thinking to help take a human-centric approach to communicating.

A part of understanding your audience is engaging with them and testing your messaging and ideas with them on a small scale before you go big. They might shred your messages to bits, as a friend Phil said. He laughed with a big belly laugh recalling U.S. politics message testing that he had run. They had proudly brought key messages to a focus group, only to have them ripped to shreds. "Tiny shreds," he said. But then small-scale testing can help you articulate your message correctly in a way that will resonate with your target audience. It is easy to think we know how others feel without testing our hypothesis. It is better to get the nasty surprise that you are wrong with a small group rather than an organizationwide backlash. One of my other friends, Steph, who works in recruitment marketing makes a point of talking with her younger target group at every opportunity, whether in the queue for an ice cream or on a bus, to better understand what is important to them and motivates them.

There is still a lot of focus in the internal communication profession on the channels your audience uses to communicate rather than looking at the needs and preferences of the organization and audience, taking more of a holistic view on how they like to communicate.

As the basic sender–receiver theory states, each channel has different characteristics to keep in mind. For example, you can achieve other things with an in-person "ask me anything" session compared to an e-mail. Always focus on your audience. Your internal communication professional can advise you on the best channel to reach them for the content you want to communicate. Every organization is different. Every target audience is different at different points in time.

Just as you would never break up with a friend via a post-it note (one would hope), you should never let people know they have lost their job via a town hall for all of the company to see. Twitter's (now called X) firing of almost half their staff in 2022 via e-mail is an example. Some staff members reported they lost access to Slack, e-mail, and other internal systems around eight hours before receiving an e-mail notifying them that they had been made redundant as a part of a layoff. One would wonder how and where they received their e-mail.

If you want more visibility over your target audience and channels, ask for a channel matrix from your communication professional. Jenni Field in her 2021 book *Influential Internal Communication: Streamline Your Corporate Communication to Drive Efficiency and Engagement*, gives a lovely, simplified example of a channel matrix. The audience and purpose of the channel is the most important piece of information, then content, frequency, lead time, and who owns it.

Getting Your Stakeholders on Board

If you have great ideas but the people around you don't support you, it is very hard to succeed. This is an essential point for getting your implementation right and should not be skipped due to lack of time. It starts before you communicate at scale and continues throughout your project, wrapping up with evaluation and recommendations as your project concludes.

This is where your stakeholders and stakeholder management come in. This is no different if you are a chief information officer (CIO) running a technology project or if you are communicating about a new culture strategy. All of the people involved need to be aligned with their roles in the project. They may be people within your organization and can also be outside of your organization, such as a regulatory body or works council, or union. I see many strategies where people confuse the target audience with the stakeholders or try to communicate with all staff without keeping the key members of the broader project team informed. Surprises for your birthday can be nice, but they're not nice when you are busy in a work environment and are sprung on you unexpectedly.

The RACI analysis (mentioned earlier) can help you articulate how to engage with different people or groups. When developing a communication strategy for a project, I'll usually ask to see the stakeholder engagement plan. If I am running the project, I'll usually put the stakeholder engagement and communication plan together so that I can make sure that no one has any nasty surprises and that I can also identify where the milestones are. For example, I ensure I have enough wriggle room and time to fix things if a senior stakeholder says no.

If you are working on technology projects, you may like to read Gartner's article on "A CIO's Framework for Communicating Strategy." They pay particular attention to the importance of stakeholder management and discuss how the stakeholders will be interested for one or more of the four following reasons:

- The stakeholders are **responsible** for getting the work done.
- They are **accountable** for the outcomes or results of the work.
- They need to be **consulted** while the work is being done.
- They need to be **informed** along the way as to the progress being achieved.

Doing this analysis and writing it up as a table is your RACI, and you should be able to ask your internal communication team to do this for you. What and when you engage and influence them depends on where they are in the RACI. I think it is important for both leaders and communicators to complete this for more complex and internally political projects. It is important to work out who is responsible for what relationships, and what is the best way to influence these people.

The order in which you communicate with your stakeholders and audiences is essential. This is why the strategy should outline timing. This should be covered in detail in the communication plan. As a leader, you should be able to scan this and make sure that:

- Employees are informed before external unless there is a legal reason for it to happen concurrently.
- Managers are informed before staff, and that they are equipped to support their staff through change.
- It is clear how each stakeholder will be approached and in which order. Who should be spoken with first to get them on board, and who would they be able to influence?
- Stakeholder interdependencies are identified. People talk. We live in a network of relationships. What risks and opportunities are associated with people talking?

Organizational Listening

Mike Pounsford, Dr. Kevin Ruck, and Howard Krais have been running an organizational listening project for many years. Organizational listening is when you listen at scale to the different people within your organization. Technology has undoubtedly made this much simpler for us in the last few years and given us even easier and quicker ways to gather and analyze data.

I spoke with Mike and Howard in 2023 about organizational listening. They said their research had shown that companies that listen perform better, especially if you get those people closest to the customer to share what they are hearing and experiencing with the customer. If you listen to your people, you'll also understand how your change programs and messaging are landing with them.

The statistically significant differences that Mike, Kevin, and Howard found, were in the positive difference that listening made in leading change. The more companies were perceived to use input from employees to improve performance, the more likely they were to see positive responses to questions about managing change, fairness, and innovation.

When they started their research, one of the things that stood out to them was how much people confuse surveys with actually listening. I've seen this myself in organizations. There is too much of a focus on response rates and employee surveys trying to represent what they've heard, rather than delving deeper into the meaning with focus groups. Another area of weakness that we succumb to is forgetting to look more broadly at the survey information and combining it with other data such as turnover rates and sick leave to give more depth and meaning. It is important to listen in and work out what is going on in those hot spots.

"So one of the barriers to organizational listening is that idea that, 'Oh well, we've conducted the survey, therefore we've listened,'" Mike said. "There's a lot more to it than that. We need to understand how people feel about things. We need to be qualitative. We need to have representative groups. There are many different ways that we should go about listening."

And it goes deeper than just understanding engagement rates. The idea that leaders have a monopoly on all the right answers simply does not make sense. It can be immensely valuable when leaders listen with an open mind to what their team members think. Listening might focus on anything from improving customer service to the way a particular change program is progressing, to finding innovative solutions to outstanding challenges. Howard suggests that many organizations are full of people bursting with the desire to do things better but ultimately frustrated when they are never asked to help or their help is not received and acted upon.

It was late at night, my time, sitting in my study in Melbourne, and early in the United Kingdom, their time. Although I felt bleary-eyed, I was fascinated at the clear link that they had found between organizational culture and organizational listening.

"You know, if you're going to listen effectively, you've got to have a culture within the organization that values and recognizes the importance of people's perspectives at all levels," Mike said. He continued:

> From the team meetings and the way we listen in team sessions to the way we do it companywide. And, that's where that thing about openness and curiosity comes in. The mindset is so important. Because, if you don't have that and you don't have a leadership group that believes in listening, then I think it's really difficult to listen well elsewhere in the business.

It is not only about listening but also about the whole process, intention, and the perception of employees around this. I talked with Ross Monaghan, CEO-turned-communication academic, trainer, and adviser, about the need not only to listen but to also follow through on the exercise. This was one of our many animated discussions, and probably over good Indian or Asian cuisine with our friend Mel. I'd just spoken with Howard and Mike a few days earlier.

Rule number one with surveys is that you need to communicate the results back in a timely and transparent way to your people. They can smell spin a mile away. Then you need to follow through on recommendations and give reasons why certain actions haven't been completed or have been delayed. The risk is not only about potentially breaking trust but also demotivating your people to complete further surveys. The same principles go for focus groups and other forms of listening when you are asking your people to invest time and energy into giving you feedback.

Ross summed it up by saying "If you listen, you also need to be open to change. If you're not open to change, pretending to listen is counterproductive."

One of the most valuable ways to listen at an organizational level is through ESNs, which we'll discuss later, and most importantly using this type of listening doesn't make any commitments to your audience. Just as your social media team will have listening tools that highlight trends, influencers, and nasty issues that arise, so can analytics for ESNs.

One of my contacts is working on and improving an AI-powered listening tool that can take all of the conversations on employee digital platforms and provide sentiment analysis, synthesizing information in multiple languages and allowing the data to be sorted by different target groups (location, etc.). Other ways to listen are to build feedback loops into your communication plan and collect and analyze data. See the measurement section coming up soon.

These points go back to understanding your audience and constantly and consistently listening to them at scale. Most importantly, it is about having that ongoing dialogue with them to create a shared understanding.

Scan to listen

Monique Zytnik podcast. "Mike Pounsford and Howard Krais talking about organizational listening," 2024. https://soundcloud.com/monique-zytnik/organisational-listening-mike-pounsford-and-howard-krais

Streamlining the Communication Experience

Over the years, I've seen streamlining internal communication becoming more important as content gets easier and quicker to produce. Streamlining means eliminating unhelpful content and putting similar content or campaigns together to create better context and more impact on employees. An excellent centralized internal communication team will understand the need to coordinate the content going out with each other and to their clients. They know they add value by being able to advise their different internal clients about what other campaigns are running and where the opportunities are. They can encourage different business areas to collaborate on similar or complementary messaging campaigns. Your message is more valuable to your people if it is put in the context of everything else that is going on around them.

Diversity, equity, and inclusion is a big topic compared to 10 years ago. It has also meant that our language has shifted to accommodate this. The number of stakeholder groups internally is huge, from the team focused on environmental, social, and corporate governance (ESG) to the different diverse networks within an organization, including neurodiversity, gender identity and preferences, and in Australia, indigenous networks. Many countries with colonial histories also have their own network groups. Then, HR teams report on company targets and run initiatives to meet metrics. Many organizations now also have employee well-being teams.

Imagine all of them wanting their airtime in an uncoordinated way. That is at least 10 different groups throwing objects at one person. Bringing these stakeholders together and creating a simple framework to help them work together can bring significant results to an organization. It will help by coordinating the messaging, channels, and campaigns. The communication professional becomes the referee or conductor, coordinating a better employee communication experience.

Measurement

Did it really happen if you can't measure it? Audience data will also give you insights into your target audience and show what they are interested in, what they are getting involved with, and what impact your communication is having.

As I learned the hard way as a physiotherapist, every organization is ultimately a business with a reason for being. If it isn't a government organization or a not-for-profit, then the reason is profit for the financial stakeholders. The purpose of your communication is to support the goals of your business, monetary or otherwise. Great measurement makes for a more effective success report that you can share with these stakeholders and gives you confidence that you are spending resources wisely.

If you'd like to brush up on your measurement, my favorite model is by fellow Australian Jim Macnamara, who is internationally recognized as a leader in the evaluation of communication and has published an Integrated Planning and Evaluation Model. It serves as the basis of evidence-based planning as well as evaluation. Integration across the process is essential, rather than trying to tack on evaluation at the end. For example, Jim always emphasizes that "early planning should include collecting baseline data (existing levels of knowledge, awareness, etc.) as well as attitudes, and so on."

I first came across this model when I met Jim at a conference in Canberra. It was one of my first speaking gigs, and I joined his preconference workshop, late from the airport, sheepishly sliding into a chair. Not only is he an excellent teacher and very generous with his ideas but his model also is highly comprehensive, taking you through looking at inputs (precomms) to measuring activities, outputs, outcomes, and impact. The idea is that you work from the left to the right, measuring inputs, activities, outputs, outcomes, and ultimately the impact of communication. Stopping measurement at vanity metrics such as follows and likes or simply measuring outputs, such as media impressions or publication circulation, robs you of pursuing the direct link to results from communication efforts.

I walked away with an A3 printout of the model, knowledge on how these areas could most effectively be measured, and a headful of ideas on how to do things better. Jim has given his permission for me to share his model with you.

If you ever come across Jim's Pink Sari case study from the Multicultural Health Communication Service (MHCS), read it. It's a beautiful example of community engagement, codesign, and evaluation that achieved outstanding results. The campaign aimed to encourage older Indian and Sri Lankan women living in New South Wales (NSW), Australia, to get mammograms to detect breast cancer early. There were several challenges, and previous advertising and media campaigns had failed. It was a community-involved campaign that included a

FOUNDATION: THE BASICS YOU CAN'T MISS 51

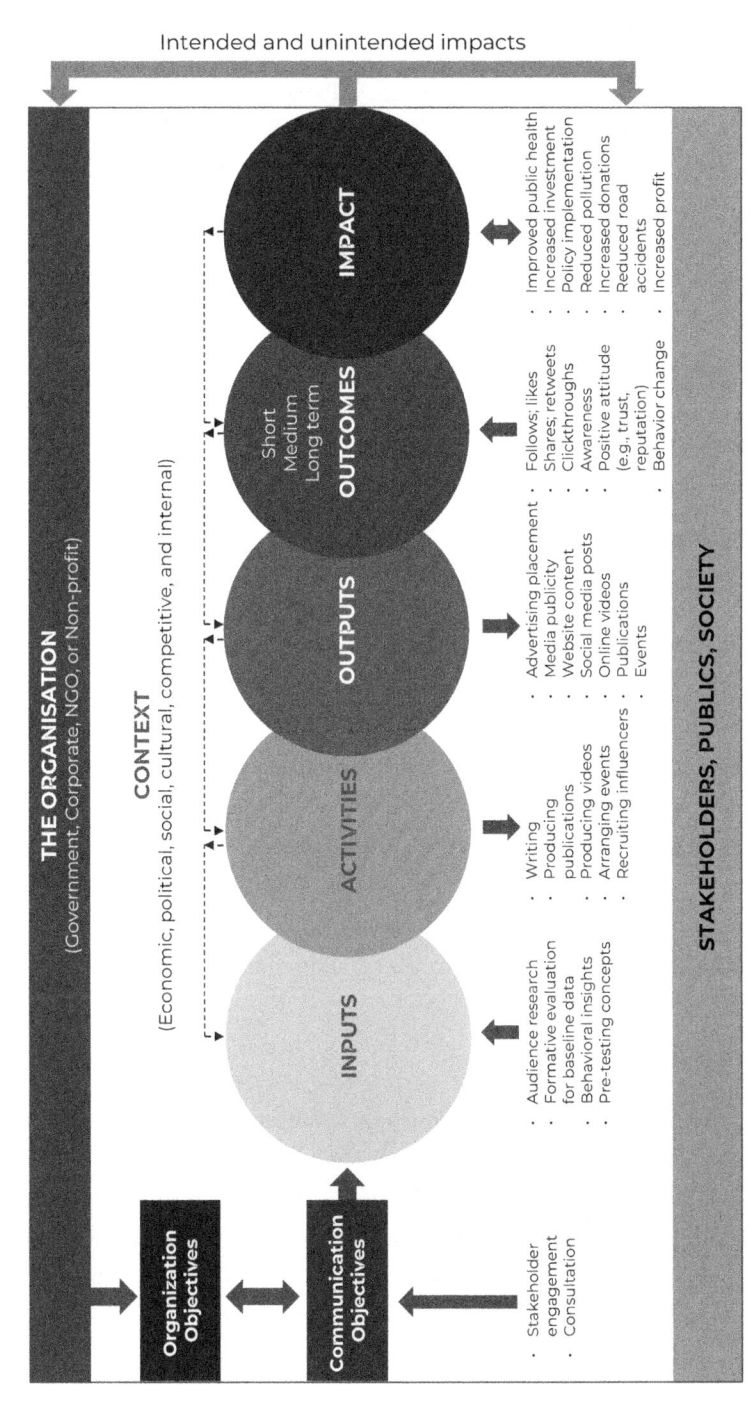

Intended and unintended impacts

THE ORGANISATION
(Government, Corporate, NGO, or Non-profit)

CONTEXT
(Economic, political, social, cultural, competitive, and internal)

Organization Objectives ↔ Communication Objectives

- Stakeholder engagement
- Consultation

INPUTS
- Audience research
- Formative evaluation for baseline data
- Behavioral insights
- Pre-testing concepts

ACTIVITIES
- Writing
- Producing publications
- Producing videos
- Arranging events
- Recruiting influencers

OUTPUTS
- Advertising placement
- Media publicity
- Website content
- Social media posts
- Online videos
- Publications
- Events

OUTCOMES
Short
Medium
Long term

- Follows; likes
- Shares; retweets
- Clickthroughs
- Awareness
- Positive attitude (e.g. trust, reputation)
- Behavior change

IMPACT
- Improved public health
- Increased investment
- Policy implementation
- Reduced pollution
- Increased donations
- Reduced road accidents
- Increased profit

STAKEHOLDERS, PUBLICS, SOCIETY

Integrated Planning and Evaluation Model, copyright Jim Macnamara, reproduced with permission.

champion network and partnerships. These techniques will be covered in the next chapter on the network effect. Outcomes of the Pink Sari campaign included an extraordinary 39 percent increase in the number of Indian and Sri Lankan women between 50 and 69 years old living in NSW having a breast screen for the first time. Health officials predicted that the impact of such increases would lead to more effective treatment of breast cancer and save lives. Through measurement across the project, we can show and know the campaign's success compared to previous attempts.

Jim has also done a lot of work on organizational listening and misinformation. His 2020 book *Beyond Post-Communication: Challenging Disinformation, Deception, and Manipulation* was timely, admittedly hefty, and well worth the read.

Risk Mitigation

What could go wrong? Plenty. Poorly communicated layoffs in 2023 and into 2024 have resulted in unsettled employees who remain in the organization. The good ones, the desirable talent, have either found new jobs or are waiting to leave once the economy stabilizes.

What is the risk of dropping the ball? What other risks are there, and what will you do to make sure these risks are minimized? In some situations, some laws cover when and to whom you can communicate specific information. For example, mergers and acquisitions have a lot of rules concerning when certain information is allowed to become public.

Accessibility

Accessibility is about making sure your communication is inclusive for everyone. While your workforce may have few people with an obvious disability, people do not always choose to, nor do they have to disclose. All corporate communication should follow best practice accessibility guidelines. For example, color contrast accessibility guidelines help to ensure that the contrast between text and background makes reading easier. Avoid having text in images and always provide "alt-text".

Table formats should be simplified to make it easier for screen readers to explain the content in documents and web pages. Unless a PDF has been expressly set up as an accessible document, it often can't be read by visually impaired people. These are just some examples. There are also guidelines for best practice communication for people with different types of neurodiversity.

Asking the right questions of your communication team including your designers can help you know if accessibility has been considered. This is becoming more important as AI develops, machine learning improves, and people with disabilities can use these tools to more easily access content.

What to Look for in an Implementation Plan

When looking at a strategy document from someone else, it can be hard to tell if all of the basics have been covered. The implementation or action plan part of the strategy will often give you clues. It should be able to be viewed in chronological order and cover how different audiences will be communicated with, who is responsible for doing this, and what the current status for each item is. The item or thing is often called a product or asset, such as a video, an event, or an e-mail.

The implementation plan can be in a Word or Excel document in a table format. It can also be in a digital card system such as Trello or MS Planner where you can map it out on a calendar and also look at it in a table format. A high-level timeline in a PowerPoint slide with pretty pictures is also okay as long as it is clear what is planned when, who will be communicated with, and most importantly, who is responsible for making it happen.

My preferred implementation plan format for complex strategies looks like the following table, because you can easily see the publish date and product on the left and the status on the far right. The table shows what information is important and how it can be organized so the information is easily understandable.

What you want to look for is that the right audiences or stakeholder groups have been communicated with, in the correct order and the way that they are being communicated with makes sense.

EXAMPLE OF TABLE FORMAT FOR IMPLEMENTATION PLAN

HOW	WHO	WHAT	RESPONSIBLE	STATUS
Product Publishing date	Specific target audience	Theme of the message and any details	Who is doing what by when	Not started/ in progress or complete Link to the draft or published final Include stats/ evaluation
Free online toolkit 1 August	All staff	Free Friday hub with links to policies, positive stories, and research. Updated weekly as the initiative progresses.	Draft & manage approvals: Cassie Walters by 22/7	26/7 Complete Unpublished
Tool kit for managers email 1 August	Managers with direct reports	Background on Free Friday initiative, link to online toolkit.	Draft: Sally-Ann Buggle by 25/7 IC to send	In progress 27/10 Draft with Karen Peters for approval
Intranet news story 6 August 2024	All staff (intranet access)	Every Friday is Free Friday. You can do what you want because we value you. Interview + photo with Bobby Bob. Link to online toolkit for more information.	Write: Peter Piper by 1/8 IC news to publish	In progress

EXAMPLES

Red Flags to Look for

If you ever see a strategy that relies on cascading information effectively or too much focus on employee engagement, consider these red flags to your internal communication aspirations of success. Put simply, if you only cascade or have employee engagement as the main feature in your strategy, I'd be surprised if you didn't fail.

Cascade

One of the most frustrating terms is "let's cascade this." A cascade is a term for information to start from the top and then be sent manager by manager to the most junior staff. It is frustrating because the idea relies on each and every person in the chain not only passing on the information but also giving it context as they pass it to the next person in the chain. It is the annoyance of many experienced communication professionals who have seen large chunks of an organization not receive information because someone along the line has not passed along the information. Shel Holtz, whom you met earlier over pastrami on rye, was of the opinion that "Anyone who has ever played the children's game of telephone knows how well communication cascades work." Telephone is where the children sit in a circle and one child whispers a secret to the next. It goes around the circle until the last person announces what the secret is. The joke of the game is that the result is rarely the same as the original message. Other internal communication experts such as David Cowan in his book *Strategic Internal Communication: How to Build Employee Engagement and Performance* call for the term to be banned and I'm with him on this one.

We now have better systems in place and can segment different organizational levels and e-mail them directly to ensure they get the information they need rather than relying on managers to pass on information. We can also target through different intranet and employee app platforms that offer content tailoring. I have been the recipient of cascaded information, and by the time I received it, I had no idea what it was about or how much it had been changed or filtered. I also often had the sneaking suspicion that it was irrelevant to me.

A better way is for the communication team to tailor the messages to each relevant employee group and then ask the responsible manager to further contextualize. A team should not need to rely on their manager's manager to pass on critical information, especially when we start to talk about asynchronous work and job-sharing situations.

Too Much Focus on Employee Engagement

Employee engagement is a measurement of the emotional commitment that an employee has to the organization and its goals. It does not mean employee happiness, satisfaction, or a psychologically safe workplace. It is a good indicator of a profitable workplace, but it should not be seen as necessarily the end result of good management. Internal communication can focus on engaging with employees on a particular topic to get a certain outcome, but from a communication perspective, it is not the end goal. In my opinion, the business reason for wanting engaged employees is that it boosts discretionary effort. Unpaid overtime is supposed to lead to higher profit margins and is therefore considered by some as good for business.

Imbalance in the Type of Channels and Content Related to the Target Audience

While some people hate reading, some people prefer written communication. Just be sure there is a balance. Anything important should be communicated in a more context-rich way such as a personal call or meeting and be followed up in a carefully thought-out, written way that can easily be scanned and digested by your people. It is always useful to know your target audience's communication channel preferences. For example, an HR expert who I met in London was exasperated by the fact that their service ticket system trigged e-mails (a job request when something needed to be done). The e-mail was sent to their frontline staff, who didn't have/use company e-mail. Someone had to go in manually and check what service requests were logged in the system and use other communication channels to reach the right frontline staff member to get the job done.

The Reward

By understanding the fundamental level of sender–receiver communication and how it is relevant today, you'll not only be able to prevent your friends and the people you love from communicating badly, but you'll also be able to make sure you are dealing with a solid communication strategy when communicating at scale. One that you can proudly share with stakeholders to get their input and buy-in, and refer to when you proudly demonstrate success.

I also like to regularly evaluate my strategies when implemented, check the numbers, get feedback, and make necessary tweaks. Just because it was right two weeks ago doesn't mean that circumstances haven't changed and that it needs to be updated.

> ### Questions to Ask to Make Sure the Basics Are Being Considered
>
> - Who are we talking with, and what do we want them to know, think, feel, and do?
> - What listening are we doing to make sure our internal communication is effective?
> - What are the situational risks and issues and how can they be mitigated?
> - What will we do if things go wrong? This is particularly important for issue or crisis communication. Remember everything internal can easily go external as well.
> - What considerations have we given to accessibility?
> - What needs to be measured? What numbers and feedback do I want to have at the end of this project when I am reporting success?

Discussion: Taking a Human-Centric Approach

I spoke with the IoIC Future of Internal Communication podcast hosts Cathryn Barnard and Dominic Walters about whether they felt that the sender–receiver model is still fit for purpose. Cat is a partner at Working the Future, a Future of Work advisory firm, helping leaders design, build, and optimize lean and agile organizations. She was also involved in Seth Godin's Carbon Almanac project.

Cat made a key point that technology has enabled a lot of our organizational communication, but that we should remember the essence of what it is to communicate and the role that this has in why people work for certain organizations.

Cat explained:

> We have this amazing opportunity now to amplify conventional internal communications, which was far more predicated on broadcast transmission of information. It now needs to be complemented by human-to-human communication, to the point where we need great ambassadors of communication within our organization who can help and facilitate and role model what human-to-human communication looks and feels like, not least as we continue to have increasing numbers of digital natives entering workplaces. So, we need to get back to the essence of what communication is and how it is the lynchpin for optimal human functioning together.

When I clarified that she meant face-to-face communication that had largely gone missing during the pandemic, Cat agreed, emphasizing: "communication that underpins trust building, relationship building, empathy, connection, a sense that we belong in our tribe, all of those things."

Dominic Walters is a specialist in communication and change, training, and development. He has worked at Lloyds Bank, Computershare, PwC, to name a few, and is a past chair of the IoIC.

Dominic talked about the shift in our approach over the years saying:

> The move from sender–receiver to a more inclusive model, if I can call it that, reflects the shift of the internal communication profession. So, there was a time, probably not that long ago in some organizations, where they called it internal marketing, which, of course, it isn't. The difference is that with internal marketing, you send out a lot of messages and hope that people will receive and understand them. The big difference with internal communication is that you have the opportunity to have regular conversations with your audience. I think that's one of the big changes we've seen.

He reflected on the role of internal communication in an organization saying:

> It's also about the role of internal communicators. It's a debate that we're still having as a profession. To what extent are we propagandists, mouthpieces for the organization? To what extent are we there to encourage conversation and be the conduit for listening? And I think the glib answer is it's a bit of both. It has to be. I mean we have to make sure that people are clear about what the organization is trying to do and why, but we also want to make sure they want to be part of it and that means they must be listened to as well. So, I think there has been a big shift.

Dominic also talked about how the internal communication role has shifted toward supporting managers being communicators. I've personally witnessed this shift, particularly after the crisis phase when a visible strong leader needed to recede and team managers had to step up and become stronger organizational communicators and sense makers for their teams.

Dominic explained:

> And I think another key part of that is the role of leaders and line managers because we used to talk about cascades and team briefs, and they were a huge step forward from what we had before. But they relied upon the line managers broadcasting as communicators. And I think now what more organizations are doing is what Cat has described in becoming more human and helping their line managers have conversations.
>
> So not necessarily broadcasting or being great in their articulation, though it's good if they can do it, but much more around asking questions, tapping into people's emotion, understanding what they're doing, helping people make sense of stuff. So, I guess now we would say if someone said "what's my job?" when it comes to communication, we'd say that it is to help your people make sense of what's going on. I think perhaps 30 to 40 years ago more people would have said it's about clarity of message, making sure

that people hear it. I think now more people are saying we need to help them understand and explain their thoughts.

If we return to my multilayered internal communication model and zoom into the foundation layer, we can see that everything else is built upon this layer. The following model shows the relationship between the concepts and types of tactics and assets/products that a communicator can use.

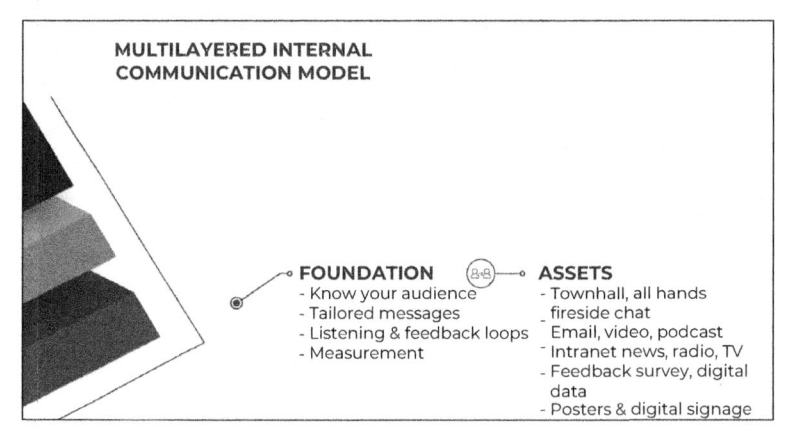

MULTILAYERED INTERNAL COMMUNICATION MODEL

FOUNDATION
- Know your audience
- Tailored messages
- Listening & feedback loops
- Measurement

ASSETS
- Townhall, all hands fireside chat
- Email, video, podcast
- Intranet news, radio, TV
- Feedback survey, digital data
- Posters & digital signage

Foundational internal communication is focused on creating a dialogue between the organization and the target audiences. There are specific tools and tactics that can help you do this.

Key Takeaways

Effective internal communication requires the basics to be done well.

- The sender–receiver model has evolved to a dialogue model.
- Know your audience.
- Organizational listening is more important than ever.
- Measurement is a basic requirement. Without it you cannot know if your communication was successful or needs to be changed.

CHAPTER 4

Multidirectional Networks

Made Easier Through Social Media

Following the launch of a six-year corporate strategy, with town halls, manager kits, and the works, we knew that we needed to engage with staff at a grassroots level and spark conversation. Internal communication worked with the culture team and creative designers to devise a campaign to highlight how people could take responsibility for doing things better. The campaign used cartoons to cut through and spark peer-to-peer conversations. The cartoons showed staff members doing things without thinking—for example, a group of people sitting around a table wondering why they were there and what the meeting was about, only to realize that the person who had called the meeting had left the organization. Other cartoons showed people e-mailing each other who were sitting next to each other to communicate, rather than having a conversation. Another showed someone watching a computer catch fire and not taking responsibility for the situation.

Draft sketch by Mike Jacobsen for the 2018 #Rethink campaign republished with permission.

[Cartoon: Four people at a meeting table with speech bubbles: "So Liz, so what's our agenda?" "Tony, you set up the meeting" "Bob asked me to do it" "Dude Bob's moved teams". Labeled "Rethink."]

Cartoon by Mike Jacobsen for the 2018 #Rethink campaign republished with permission.

As the campaign's strategist, in addition to the advertising style campaign using our internal channels, I ensured that the overarching messages were woven through intranet news stories and other employee communications. My favorite news story was a question-and-answer format of a very senior and engaging leader, Frances Cawthra. She talked about the bigger strategy launch and the importance of stopping and evaluating if what you were doing made sense. She said:

> Our thinking can get lost in dollars and accounts, and we all need to step back and look at the bigger picture. We need to be thoughtful about how and where we are using our resources. Are we streamlined? We need to think about things at the grassroots level.

"If I were making this decision for me, with my money, for my purpose, would I think it is value for money? Would the people I think most highly of say, yes, that was a great decision?"

"At the town halls, I have seen our staff talking about grassroots ideas—how can I get the basics done brilliantly every time. It is the cornerstone for operational excellence, and also building trust and confidence."

Frances also shared that she enjoyed riding her motorbike with her partner on the weekend and spending time with her granddaughter. I still remember our telephone interview in the prevideo days. The staff loved the article, especially the photo of her on her Indian Chieftain motorbike with her partner, and our readership went nuts. We had over double the average number of page views for the article and plenty of comments on Viva Engage (this ESN was called Yammer at the time), which had just switched from being a pilot project to being available for all staff to use.

Using Viva Engage to create a cross-organizational community that could connect in real-time was a key part of this campaign and something that wouldn't have been previously possible.

As it was still a new channel for corporate communication at the time, the first few posts were neutral and hesitant. As the campaign progressed, we started to ask staff what annoyed them, and what they thought could be done more efficiently or better. Because I'd designed an agile campaign, we were able to take the discussions on Viva Engage and reflect them back into the traditional all-staff channels such as the intranet news. We also started to embed the Viva Engage community into the end of the articles on the intranet so staff would be curious and join the conversation. Through sparking conversation on Viva Engage, there were 21 new initiatives that the staff identified and were captured as a part of organizational change to be implemented.

It was a six-week campaign that ended by clearly handing the responsibility to our staff members to make change. Quite often, good practitioners try to do this with their campaigns but we don't always expect our campaigns to grow legs and run.

What surprised me the most about the #Rethink campaign was that four months later I started to get e-mails from people asking if I had been involved in or had known about different initiatives they had seen—they had forwarded me e-mails and news articles coming from across the organization. Different areas of the business such as HR and the security department had started to do their own reviews or initiatives, looking at how they could make small changes around themselves. They were using the rethink language of our campaign and showed that they owned the change. This campaign's impact on the organization was tangible and incredible, considering it all started with a few funny cartoons.

We were finalists in Australia's Mumbrella CommsCon Awards Best Internal Communication in 2019 and 2020 and global Gartner Awards

Finalists in the Employee Engagement category in 2020. I've presented this case study at several conferences and shifted the perception of employee communication as boring and unengaging. When it is fun and quirky and your people have a chance to get involved at scale and be a part of the discussion, you'll find your networks and communities buzz and take on a life of their own.

The original idea had been inspired by an Australian rail company's 2012 public safety campaign Dumb Ways to Die, which used cartoons and tongue-in-cheek humor to talk about challenging topics. Dumb Ways to Die was the most awarded communication campaign in the history of Cannes (with 28 Lions, including 5 Grand Prix) and over 127 million people have stated that they would be safer around trains because of the campaign.

When I think back to our #Rethink campaign, it is hard to believe how the ESN helped to quickly build a community in the organization, and it is a community that evolved and effectively functioned for further campaigns supporting the corporate strategy.

Building or Tapping Into Networks

Within an organization, your organization, think about all of the networks that you know about. You may have a network of executive assistants who meet regularly, and provide mentorship and training for their network or you could have more social ones such as a local LGBTI+ community network. An office I worked in had a knitting network where colleagues would meet at lunchtime and knit together. They would display and sell their beautiful handmade creations in the foyer for special events. It is about people connecting and coming together with shared interests. This social glue helps strengthen information sharing and culture across the organization and is usually driven by the people.

It is interesting to note that a common stand against someone or something can also form strong communities and we should keep this in mind when considering communication strategies and risks.

Technology, such as ESN platforms and apps, has made building communities so much easier and communication within the network faster. It lets you break down rank and give a voice to the employee. Some of these platforms or products can integrate into intranets or digital workspaces to make access and collaboration almost seamless for your people. This is why network technology has become an easy addition to communication strategies—simple and easy for internal communication professionals to engage with the right community online and see how they respond to the conversation.

The common trait with networks is that they cross business units and teams, locations, functions, or all of them, and are made up of people. This is important because it is about social connectivity. Think of it more like a team sport rather than a game of catch.

It is more than communicating; it is about building relationships and interdependencies.

You can build your network for a specific purpose or tap into existing ones. Because it is about people, your approach should always be respectful. You are building or entering a community with its own intent, culture, and etiquette. High-functioning networks will focus on longevity, trust-building within the network, and clear purpose.

From my experience, this means the following:

- Because of the focus on trust—feedback from the communities is valuable.
- If employees support your ideas and projects, your message will spread.
- Networks can cross locations, job functions, and teams, which means that you can bypass blockers, such as the senior manager who doesn't support your project and deliberately keeps their team and the people below them uninformed. Tapping into a community that crosses into this area can help you cut through to that area of the business.
- Because they are people-focused, networks can be messy.
- Communities take time and investment to build and maintain. Be clear on what resources you have and how long you are committing to if you are considering building your own.

If you are interested in reading more about the benefits of communities and the networking effect, I'd recommend looking into Seth Godin's work on tribes and ideas that spread. He has a number of books such as *Tribes: We Need You to Lead Us* (2008) and a great podcast called Akimbo that you can listen to on any podcast catcher.

Why Understanding Networks Is Important

What we see outside of organizations, we also see inside of organizations. Technology, such as those used for ESNs, has made connections between people easier.

If you don't understand the principles of networks, you risk causing confusion and delay as Thomas the Tank engine would say (did I mention I have two boys?). At best, your personal reputation will suffer; at worst, a group of people in the community can turn around and attack, causing internal reputational damage that goes externally with the flick of an e-mail or a phone call.

Working with communities can not only be powerful but also dangerous if you walk blindly into them.

The example that is being bandied about in the reputation area of communication is the Bud Lite example from April 1, 2023, where they misjudged their audience and partnered with a transgender influencer, causing divisions in communities and violent threats against employees of Bud Lite. The company was trying to nurture the LGBTI+ community but didn't fully understand their customer base. They admit that their strategy wasn't well thought out.

If we look at the external communication world, working with influencers has become commonplace as a part of an organization's marketing strategy. When talking with the influencer management lead at Siemens, a global technology company, there has been a shift from paying influencers to promote a product or company, to treating them in more of a traditional media relations way. This means giving the influencers priority access to information before other people or giving them access to top researchers or people in the company. Information has become the currency, and I see this model also playing out in internal champion networks within organizations. Interestingly, some organizations are already starting to establish paid influencer roles within the organization. For example, at a 2024 IntraTeam event, one of the presenters spoke about how the influencer's role was to share relevant IT tips and engage with employees on their ESN to help people better understand the technology within the company.

For many change management projects such as new technology adoption, champion networks are set up to help spread the word within the organization and to support others through change. The strategy reflects the concept that people will trust peers sometimes more than leaders.

Employer Branding Is the Perfect Example of Where to Use Networks

As internal communication has moved toward activating employees outside of the workplace channels, so has the prominence of employer branding risen to embrace the concept of communities and the duality of internal and external communication. Employer branding is the marketing and reputation management of the entire employment experience and reflects the employee value proposition (EVP), which is the value you get when you work for a specific company. The employer brand is different from your consumer brand, but in our connected world, they interact.

I am embarrassed to say that I was rubbish at my first employer branding project. We had a fancy agency onboard. All I can remember is that their office was a strange dark green color. I think the company was named after a vegetable. Their head designer insisted on presenting, in person, artwork printed out on a hardback black card. I kept getting annoyed because I just wanted them to e-mail it to me. Each iteration seemed to be a slight change in the logo placement or a tweak in a graphic line. I let my frustrations blindsight me to the fact that I hadn't really understood our target audience outside of the organization, who we wanted to attract or how we were reaching them. I was working with marketing and the HR team, but hadn't informed myself beyond that the employer branding would be used on job ads and internally on our printed newspaper and intranet. I don't know how the campaign went because I didn't ask to see the measurement. Where you have internal and external come together, using networks is the perfect solution because it crosses divides. I think Facebook was freshly developed at that time, so perhaps this is the excuse I'll use, but it really isn't a good one.

With subsequent companies, I used networks better for employer branding, including working with our internal minority groups to encourage our employees to reach out to people who they thought would be a good fit for our company.

In the war of talent that is going on today, you can't afford to ignore employer branding. You want to attract the right people who can add value to your organization. Employer branding is the way that employers can show to the people who aren't working for them yet, what it is like to work for them. But it isn't just advertising, a video, or a few billboards. It is the whole experience including the company's reputation as an employer.

When I talk about employer branding it isn't just marketing. It needs that element of understanding the target audience and really appealing to them, bringing the EVP to life. What people are looking for has shifted so much since Covid-19, not only among the younger generation but also among more mature employees. We see this played out in the Great Resignation and Quiet Quitting. For example, research shows that people, and in particular GenZ, have personal values and now want more than just pay or flexible working conditions. Our maturing workforce is motivated by different things, where knowledge-sharing opportunities and flexibility play a role. What attracts people now isn't the same as before, and I can't tell you what will attract people to a specific role in your organization because it depends on who you are trying to recruit. Do you want a superstar, a rock star, or emerging star? Someone who will shoot ahead to success, be there to keep things stable and knowledge share, or who will grow into a role, and contribute on other fronts to the team such as culture?

Every piece of communication, from how the job description is written to the application experience, impacts whether the right applicant will even apply for the job. This is where the employer brand goes beyond communication to the experience. We almost need to draw a dotted line from here to the next chapter on immersive communication. There is a second dotted line to both alignment and leadership communication, where what you say, what you do, and what others say about you can build or destroy trust and build or eat away at your employer brand.

The foundation of the employer brand, onboarding process, and everything related to the experience of the people working for your organization, needs to be founded in good audience research and solid company policy. Good communication can help, and creative communication can inspire; but bad leadership practices, missing policies, misalignment, lack of resources, and budget or half-baked projects can't be fixed through communication alone.

How to Be Successful

You need to have the basics of a communication strategy in place. From this, you can see what kinds of networks you can build into your plan, and most importantly, if they are necessary.

Create Employee Personas to Help You Identify Which Communities to Engage With

Sometimes it might be obvious which communities your target audience belongs to, but if you need more depth, understanding your audience better will help you make the right choices.

Something we've stolen from marketing is breaking down your audience to a handful of types of representative people you are trying to reach. Giving them names, making avatars, and defining who they are and what they are interested in, allows you to visualize them when crafting messages or working out how to reach them. You can have a look on the Internet for some simple templates. They usually combine demographics (circumstances, backgrounds), psychographics (worldview, motivation), and sociographics (social networks).

There are also many models that are useful in defining the personas. I've seen Edward de Bono's Six Hats thinking model used to help a marketing team define what a specific audience is interested in. For example, do they love processes or are they more feelings-driven people? AI-powered persona modeling is already on the market and are interesting to play with. Just be careful with the built-in biases that can be present in AI-generated models.

As tempting as it is to stereotype in broad brushstroke ways, I recommend having research commissioned for creating your personas. Social scientist Walter Lippmann coined the phrase "stereotypes" in 1921 when he described why people so easily imagine how other people are, based on assumptions. It is also helpful to keep this in mind when using personas and acknowledge that not all people act or think in the same way.

You often can find the communities your people are engaging with outside of your organization. Their conversations about your organization could even be publicly available on social media. Don't discredit this method as an option for your internal communication, bringing the external back into the organization. It shows that you are listening to your people and what is important to them. You're going back to strengthening your communication foundation.

Be Clear on What You Want From the Community When You Engage With Them

Engage with purpose. Don't waste their time. Listen to what their feedback is and act on it.

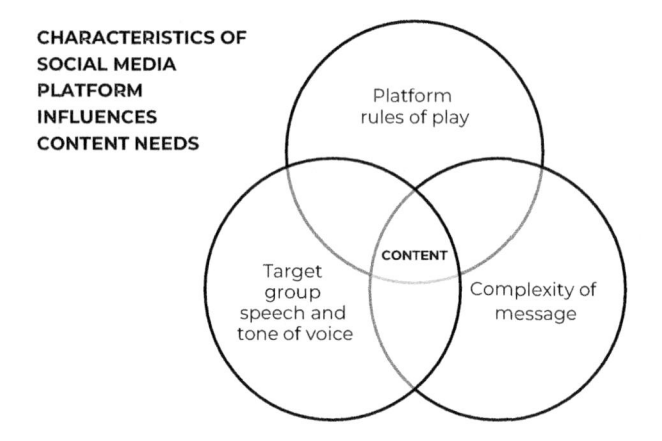

CHARACTERISTICS OF SOCIAL MEDIA PLATFORM INFLUENCES CONTENT NEEDS

- Platform rules of play
- Target group speech and tone of voice
- Complexity of message
- CONTENT

If you are creating content for the community, this model nicely explains the dynamic of the content, and how it is influenced by the rules of play on the platform, the tone and voice of your target audience, and the complexity of the message you are trying to convey.

Know Who Your Champions Are Within the Community

You'll need a key connection to invite you into the community. Add them to your stakeholder list and make sure they feel that you are respecting their time. I always find it helpful to share my ideas with them and see if they can give me insights on how to best frame my communication before I speak with the rest of the group.

It is important to know who the influencers are in the community. I am sure you've heard this many times. They may not be the most senior people, but they are the people who are vocal and that others listen to. I remember Mike Klein once telling me that it is the 3 percent rule. If you can reach them in the organization and get them to support your initiative, then you can reach most of your organization through their influence. The challenge is of course identifying the 3 percent. Organizational listening on your ESN can help identify these people. Asking your target group who they would go to for information also helps identify who the influencers are.

Join the Conversation

Bring the right people into the conversation and make sure you or the right person participates in the conversation. Be respectful that others are entitled to a different view and expect respect from them in return. Usually, an organization's general code of conduct or cultural guidelines will cover this online environment and there is no need to create new guidelines specifically for the online community. If the existing guidelines are insufficient, or need more clarity, I would strongly recommend getting the overarching guidelines updated rather than creating something additional, which could cause confusion.

If You Built the Community, You Need to Invest in the Community

It has taken companies many years to realize that social media is not free. You need to pay someone to manage it, curate the content, and facilitate the conversations. There are many platforms and tools they can use, in the same way that an internal communication professional would use ESNs.

Every Community Needs a Community Manager

In the business world, they're usually called community managers, but their role is more to facilitate, do behind-the-scenes administration, and be the point of contact between the organization and the community.

For example, the toy library committee that I was on had a chair and an admin assistant to keep the committee and broader community engaged. In the same way, best practice ESN organizations have community managers, and even my mum's bush dancing group has a president. All of these people are responsible for ensuring a clear direction and oversight, and determining that the communities are meeting their purpose. Even social media platforms are expected to provide guidelines and monitor appropriate behavior. An ESN is no different, and an organization needs to invest in a professional to manage this.

Integrate the Information Back Into the Organization

Spend time investing in taking the information out of the communities and sharing it with the right people. If you don't do this, you risk having conversation bubbles. Also, as previously mentioned, encourage your internal communication team to consider taking external conversations such as on LinkedIn, where your employees are involved and bringing it back into the internal channels. It will help senior leaders around you understand the value of the communities, regardless of the platform (analytics are great for this, too). It will also show your people that you are paying attention and listening to their conversations in a meaningful way.

Payoff for Respectfully Creating and Engaging With Communities

Effectively engaging with existing communities or creating your own helps you get around relying on all staff communication or managers to pass on information. Using communities is a technique used in external communication and is advocated widely. It is a concept that we should be applying to internal communication when it makes sense.

Don't underestimate the time and resources needed to engage with or create communities to support your communication goals. If we look to external communication, a number of roles in marketing exist to specifically manage influencers in communities. Recent years have also brought significant investment in social media professionals and social media listening tools, who are experts in interacting with communities. Community managers also exist in physical spaces, such as co-working environments.

The payoff is being able to understand and interact with your audience in the right way.

Questions to Ask to Determine How Communities Can Best Be Used for Internal Communication

- Why is it necessary to build or be a part of this community? What does it offer?
- What is important to the community? What brings them together?
- Who are the key influencers in the community? Do we need to find out?
- What additional resources are needed to manage or maintain the relationship with the community?
- What results do I expect to see from this time, resource, and financial investment?

Case Study: Facilitating Conversations for Business Outcomes

I wasn't surprised to read that ANZ bank was top in Swoop Analytics 2022/23 Yammer and Viva Engage Benchmarking Report for large-size organizations worldwide. The benchmarking report analyzed more than 21 million Yammer and Viva Engage interactions from 4.7 million employees and conducted a deep dive into 3,200 communities across 97 organizations. ANZ is one of Australia's big four banks with a presence across Australia, New Zealand, Asia, Europe, North America, and the Middle East.

I had met Ryan Crocker, Adoption and Communications Lead, ANZ, and Richard Cartmell who was the Viva Engage and Digital Channels Adoption Manager in late 2019, and had been impressed at how they had set up and managed their communities. They were working with a good friend of mine and a highly respected communication professional, Alethea Reid. Ryan and Ricky came to speak with an organization I was working with and gave us a peek into best practices. Through the Swoop platform, they were able to see how the people in their communities and networks interacted and were able to get additional metrics such as who were the influencers and how their leaders were performing.

Ryan explained:

If it's an employee sharing a personal experience, a perspective or opinion on something, it works really well. Some recent conversations that generated a lot of engagement have included a banker who shared a story about a customer who came into a branch with a unique situation, and the banker talked about how they were able to make a significant difference for that customer. Another was a powerful personal story about mental health and wellbeing—that one really resonated with our employees.

"All that kind of content just goes nuts. It shows that our employees really value the opportunity to hear and share stories and engage directly with their peers."

"Yammer (Viva Engage) creates a strong sense of community and connection. Now that we're not connecting physically in our workplaces as often, I think people are increasingly looking for digital ways to bridge that gap."

This is a great example of an organization investing in building and managing communities for collaboration, innovation, and organizational listening.

The communication professional's role in networks becomes more as the facilitator of conversation rather than the source of directive top-down communication.

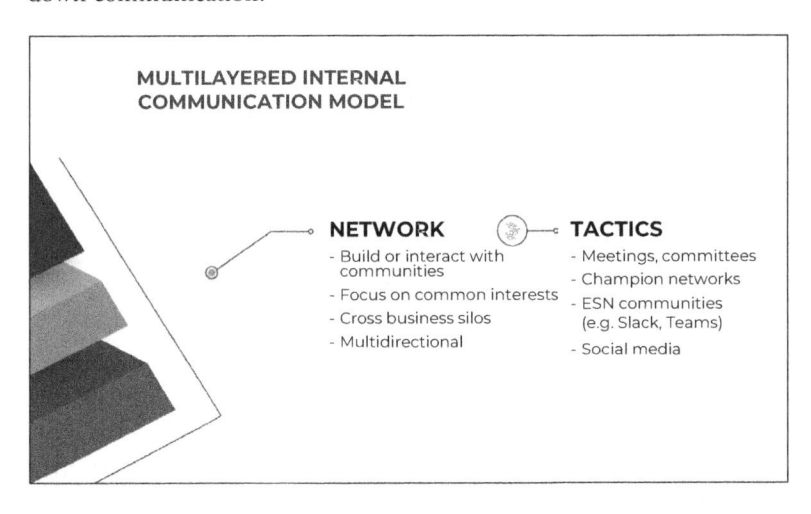

MULTILAYERED INTERNAL COMMUNICATION MODEL

NETWORK
- Build or interact with communities
- Focus on common interests
- Cross business silos
- Multidirectional

TACTICS
- Meetings, committees
- Champion networks
- ESN communities (e.g. Slack, Teams)
- Social media

Networks are formed by people with common interests with the channels and methods involved being part of the network. A sign-up element or participation needs to be a part of being "in the club."

> ## Key Takeaways
>
> We are all connected with other people. This sense of belonging is important to our well-being at work.
>
> - Nurturing communities and breaking organizational silos is important for improving the information flow, helping with culture, and strengthening the organization.
> - Management needs to feel comfortable with staff having discussions. If they don't happen online, they will happen offline.
> - Measurement of communication success is still essential.
> - Digital communities are great ways to listen without setting expectations.
> - Social media is not free—investment is needed when interacting with these communities.

CHAPTER 5

Immersive Communication

It's Not About the Technology, It Is About People and Persuasion

Only recently I discovered that my brother Lachlan used to work down the hall from Nokia Research Lab guru Tapani Levola in Finland. I visited my brother back in 2010 and walked through the gorgeous green, sweet fragranced forests near Tampere; heard his stories about sauna rooms next to meeting rooms at Nokia; and shared in his delight that he was encouraged to take breaks and go to the gym during the workday when he wasn't feeling creative. But, I hadn't actually known what he did for work, except that he had seven patents related to 3D imaging or holograms, or perhaps something to do with how we see images on flat screens. When Lachlan and I talked even more recently about immersive communication and discussed content for this book, my brother shared with me that Tapani's work on near-to-eye displays likely contributed to the technology that Microsoft's HoloLens is based on. This type of headset technology integrates the digital world into the real world based on location and objects. It is an example of immersive technology.

Immersive technology aims to substitute or blend the physical environment with a virtual content. It includes VR, where your digital environment replaces your physical surroundings. A VR headset completely restricts your vision to a digital world; haptic sensors in controllers give you physical feedback from your digital world, and spatial sound through the headset gives you the sense that you know where different objects are in the digital world. In augmented reality (AR), the virtual and physical worlds are blended. For example, you can look through a digital device such as a smartphone or tablet and see graphics superimposed over a live stream of the physical environment. The AR industry's ideal is to create slim AR glasses that can be used as an everyday item, replacing the smartphone. Films such as Spider-Man: No Way Home (2021), Ready Player One (2018), and Free Guy (2021) already idealize these possibilities, and commercial products along these lines are becoming more feasible, such as the Ray-Ban Meta smart glasses.

But this chapter isn't about the technology.

So far, we've successfully avoided the specifics of the technology. We haven't talked too much about the products or specifications because the products change from year to year and now month to month, even daily. I also know that many organizations aren't using immersive technology for employee communication, yet. In mid-2022, I did a quick scan and had 50 internal communication professionals globally report back that only three used immersive technologies for internal communication, one of which had a business interest in VR. Cost, organization readiness, and skills of their people to implement the technology were the most significant barriers. Lack of demand from the organization at the time was also high on the list of reasons for nonimplementation. I believe that the main reason for the delay is because immersive technology isn't yet a society-wide mass-adopted technology. Organizational technology tends to lag behind what is used in personal life. I also believe that Internet connection and speed in many countries are limiting the immersive experience that can be delivered to employees.

> My feeling is that you have to have a solid strategy in place first and be clear on what you're trying to achieve, or the immersive technology may end up being an expensive experiment.
> —Survey respondent

And, as my fellow communication professionals point out, strategy is the starting point. The different mechanisms of how immersive technology will be achieved, and the tactics that are used, such as an AR photo competition (best photo created with the AR app) or creating a VR game with learning modules, depend on what you're trying to achieve with the tactic.

Most people responding to the survey were unlikely to explore immersive technology in the next few years from an internal communications perspective. However, there was much agreement that VR was ideal for safety training and other forms of training.

> I believe in immersive communication and the metaverse—it is just not a thing yet or only for very few. First, we need to use it in our personal life before it will be used internally.
> —Kurt Kragh Sørensen, IntraTeam

Kurt runs great digital workplace peer-to-peer events in the Nordic region, both in person and online. He is in the European time zone and is primarily focused on global companies. I've known him for some time now and always appreciated his dry wit and considered him as one of those digital employee experience experts with their finger on the pulse—someone whose opinion I trust.

There was a high sentiment in my touchpoint survey that some immersive experiences could be created without technology. A perfect example is a physical event, where the principles can be applied to the experience. This is something I strongly agree with.

This chapter is about the people and concepts, rather than specific technologies. This is because, in the past, when technology enabled or enhanced different ways of communicating, it has influenced what is expected and social preferences for communication. When we rub away the shine of fancy technology, it all comes down to people. It still comes down to understanding and influencing people, and what their experience is.

We've covered the foundational dialogue model and networked communication. Our next level is immersive. It doesn't need fancy technology such as VR, mixed reality, AR, or holograms, but these technologies can make it easier to create a more frictionless experience for communication in the digital world, and the digital world is scalable.

The concepts covered in this chapter can be applied to internal communication strategies regardless of what immersive technology is available. As a comparable example, foundational concepts can be used without e-mail, for example, by sending a letter or leaving a note on someone's desk.

What It Looks Like: Immersive Communication Without the Technology

When I attended a 2022 event in Melbourne curated by Mykel Dixon, I knew that the corporate world was ready to think about immersive communication.

None of us knew what the event was about before we went. We just had a date, time, and address. We met in preallocated small groups at different designated cafés beforehand to connect and find a way to the venue, which was thankfully within walking distance. This preevent meeting had been orchestrated as a part of the event. If you think of a typical conference with the stage at the front with theater or cabaret-style seating, this event was set up completely different.

The chairs, sofas, and bits and pieces were arranged in concentric circles facing the center. There was no PowerPoint screen; instead, a band was set up at the circle's edge to provide spontaneous entrance music. To the side and in different rooms off the main space, there were activities that you could do whenever you wanted. You could paint a car with messages from the day (or whatever you liked) or write a letter of advice to an anonymous person at the event that would later be sent to them. There was a fun photo booth.

The speakers were all high caliber, and loosely organized into three sections. What struck me the most was that, toward the end, a scent specialist talked with us about the importance of smell. Unbeknown to us, different scents had been released during the day to help create the atmosphere in the room.

It was a powerful event that deliberately covered many of the elements of immersive communication. The explorative aspect of the event appealed to many of the senior leaders who were there, who had sat through many conventional conferences. The music and spontaneity added an element of surprise. The credible speakers, such as Aaron McEwin, VP, of Research and Advisory from Gartner, gave it that knowledge element. Because the event was so experiential and carefully curated with many communication touch points before, during, and afterward, it also created a community. This is what got me thinking about all the immersive communication ideas that I'd been developing since working on the DHL Virtual Strategy House and how they fit together with a bigger, multilayered model. It also reminded me of the value of focusing on the experience. A year later, I cannot remember the details of what was said, but a few key moments and ideas are still clear in my mind. I cannot say the same for some of the other events I've been to over the years. The stickiness of the experience simply wasn't there in many of my previous events, and my memories of them are only of exhaustion, too much information, too many people, and too much of the same content.

Immersive Communication

Immersive communication occurs when you put your audience at the center of your experience. A human-centric approach aligns with many of the current theories in human resources, from remote work to how to construct learning and development programs.

The main thing to remember is that it is experience-based.

So, through my work with immersive technologies, Andreas Ringsted and I identified three key dimensions of immersive communication. Andreas comes more from a technology background, and I took a communication perspective as we fleshed this out.

The three dimensions of immersive communication are nonlinear, multisensory, and interactive. We'll discuss these in more detail further on in this chapter.

My ideas came from the discomfort I felt when working on my first content design project for a corporate 3D space, the DHL Virtual Strategy House. I quickly discovered that there needed to be a consistent path that users would take when consuming content in the space. Using audio suddenly became important. I used this to my advantage and deliberately chose a range of voices from different countries to add an international flavor to the space. Interactivity became more critical because once you are in the area, you want to do something, not just look.

As mentioned, during lockdown, my boys would sit on my lap at the end of the day and as a treat, look at the space that I was content creating for. They could navigate and explore freely, look at things, click on things, watch videos, and do whatever caught their attention. As you can see, I started the user testing early, and unknowingly, they were helping me to design something that felt special. Any parent with a child who likes gaming (*socken* as it is called in Germany) can appreciate what the communication expectations of their children will be like when they enter the workforce in 10 years. I also gained clarity on every individual's need to have the opportunity to play to learn—though I get the feeling that some of us including me, feel like we've forgotten how to do this.

Why Should We Care About Immersive Techniques?

The art of immersive communication can be powerful for communication and persuasion. And, when the technology is available for us to use in the workplace—and this may be a form or evolution of the immersive technology available right now—we need to be ready to use it. Understanding immersive communication will also be helpful in understanding what younger generations expect. For example, a poorly printed copy of a textbook page with blanks to fill in certainly doesn't cut the mustard anymore. This painful disconnect was obvious in the type of homework my boys received during the lockdown in 2020.

If your strategy is to persuade, then immersive communication helps people accept messages and be open to other ideas more easily. It makes communication more memorable, helps people focus, and maybe helps them be more open to sharing ideas and coming up with better ways to do their jobs. It is about reducing the friction between the message and the receiver; and when done well it can border on subliminal communication, where people feel like they are experiencing, rather than being communicated with.

Learn From Other Professions

We should always look over the fence and see what others are doing so we can learn. Some of my favorite events are when I meet with other communication professionals or businesspeople and learn about how they perceive a challenge. It is like looking at different angles of a diamond.

Immersive communication is about influencing a person's experience and environment. Many of these techniques are already used by marketers and advertisers. Think of the delicious bakery smell and eye-watering, gorgeous display of donuts that makes you want to buy one (or more).

If you want to see a pro in action, watch Derren Brown trick advertisers at their own game. Derren invited two agency advertisers to his office and tasked them with creating a logo for his imaginary business. Unbeknown to them, Derren had littered their journey from the airport with prompts and clues—such as a group of kids crossing the road with the logo on their sweaters and posters in alleyways with slogans. It was uncanny to see the logo the advertisers designed compared with Derren's "ideas" that he had left on the table in a sealed envelope at the start of his briefing. He revealed his ideas after the advertising experts had presented theirs. Subliminal messaging had worked.

It was at my brother Lachlan's suggestion that I looked up Derren's video as well as the virtual barber shop, where audio recording techniques make it feel like you are getting a buzz cut when you listen and you can hear the electric shaver zooming around your head. After ongoing discussion, today I finally discovered that my brother worked in the immersive communication team at Nokia Research Labs. It had only taken me 15 years to find out. He couldn't tell me much due to age-old nondisclosure agreements (NDAs), but it was about the immersive technology (and not the theory we are discussing now). We discussed how the impact is related to how much influence you have over the experience and environment. The more control, the more power and ability to shape experience. Immersive technology makes immersive communication easier, because you have more environmental control. As the technology improves, just as we saw Facebook go from a clunky platform to an integrated product, we will see more control over the experience.

There are also ethical considerations. Should you let people know what you're doing? I recently wrote a chapter on "Getting Colleagues Comfortable With AI: A Human-Centered Approach to Technology in Organizations" with Matthew Lequick, for Quadriga University's publication on *Artificial Intelligence in Public Relations and Communication: Cases, Reflections, and Predictions*, edited by Ana Adi. Ana has always been a great sounding board for me in the communication field and is equally a big fan of Jim Macnamara's work. Ana is a great presenter and never shy to challenge the status quo.

In regard to this chapter, some of the feedback I got from reviewers was whether I should be writing about how to persuade people to use technology they weren't too keen on using. There are ethical questions in all areas of marketing and communication. The purpose of communication is often to persuade and motivate—without crossing the line into unethical manipulation.

Internal communication aims to inform, engage, or influence people within your organization about something. Of course, there are ethics involved. However, there are no hard or fast rules. As individuals, we are all different. Always start with company rules and guidelines as you will be judged by your employers against them. Be sensitive to your moral compass and as a leader question others when you believe something to be unethical. Don't let evil fester.

Our Younger Generations Are Growing Up With New Technology

Our challenge as communicators, specifically internal communicators, is that our audience's expectations have changed. When I went to school, we sat at wooden desks, in rows, facing the front with a lid at the top to put our books, pens, and pencils inside. We had special three-row lined paper to practice our cursive writing in pencil so that we could erase any mistakes. We rote-learned our timetables. I learned to type on typewriters in year eight and still had to memorize our science and math formulas for our exams in our final year.

Now my two primary school boys do learning modules on the computer at school during class. When we were back in Australia and isolating early in 2021 because we had caught Covid-19 (back when legally you had to isolate), my boys happily spent a few hours a day playing Reading Eggs. This is an online program designed to teach reading and phonetics. The graphics are good. There are great sounds, explosions, and activities for the kids to do as they climb the levels, getting points that they can spend on furniture, pets, and all sorts of strange things for their virtual house in the game. My youngest said, "It's like they got into my brain and know exactly what I like." It was a much better experience than the printed worksheets given at a different school.

This is what we're competing with.

Prepare for the Future

Using an immersive communication mindset, we will be prepared for when the technology becomes available.

Now, most employees have smartphones. Smartphones are always with you, and companies have released employee apps to go on staff personal mobile phones. Because people often have so many competing apps on their phone with excellent user experience, we need our company apps to also be of a certain standard. The experience we give workers has to keep up with what they are experiencing in their personal life and current expectations. AR with smartphones is already being used for commercial marketing. Big brand furniture stores now have apps where you can superimpose different furniture in your room at home by looking through your phone and selecting the furniture you want to display. AR is also being used as a part of internal communication campaigns. You just need a concept, developers, and integration into your existing digital landscape.

As communicators, we must be wary of using technology for technology's sake. As one of my survey respondents said:

> We have used an unreal-based virtual exhibition and mixed media conferencing. Both were highly impactful because they put the needs of the audience first. The key is understanding why the audience will want to engage with the content—the objective of the experience must deliver something they will value. It is easy to get carried away with creative ideas and extra features that add nothing (except cost and development time!) Unless the end user is put first, from both content and user experience perspectives, the immersive experience will fail to deliver against its objectives.
> —Kevin Chapple, Head of Channels and Content, Employee Communications, RS Group

I have seen content designs for 3D spaces with large walls covered in text-based posters to inform and educate the audience. There were footstep marks on the floor to show you how to walk from one display to the next. Luckily it didn't get built. I say this because it would have been equivalent to having posters on the wall in a science museum instead of a series of interactive, well-considered multimedia displays. They were completely missing the opportunity for an immersive experience that is nonlinear, interactive, and gamified.

The Three Dimensions of Immersive Communication

The easy way to make your strategy more immersive is to ensure that it includes the three dimensions of being nonlinear and interactive and appeals to as many senses as possible. I find it helpful to think of it like the following model.

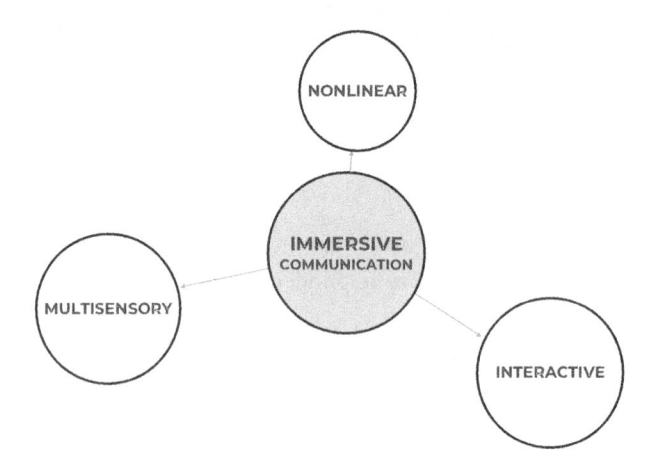

Nonlinear

Imagine yourself in an art gallery. You can go left; you can walk right; you can go to the back of the room and hop from one piece to the next, depending on what catches your eye. Some people will read every piece of information and listen to the audio descriptions, whereas others will sit in front of whatever inspires them the most and contemplate. The joy of an art gallery is that everyone takes something away from it. The collection together needs to make sense, as do the individual pieces as stand-alone. The lighting is also essential, as are the ambient sounds. The viewer has the freedom to pick and choose.

Nonlinear communication does not rely on an employee being in the office and consuming content in a time-linear way, as the order of consumption is flexible. Nor does it mean that the same message needs to be plastered across all channels until your people are bored.

Interactive

For anyone who has children or loves LEGO, exploring LEGO House in Denmark is at the top (or near the top) of the experience bucket list. It's like visiting your favorite old-school sweet shop that is bright and colorful with so much to look at and be fascinated by. But it's more than this. Based in Billund, 165 miles (250 km) west of Copenhagen, Denmark is the giant Lego brick-looking structured palace. I wasn't surprised to learn of the planning, thought, detail, and trailing that went into creating the perfect experiences in each zone. The foundation or core of the approach was the Lego Foundation's learning-through-play philosophy. Every experience was carefully thought through to allow for self-discovery and interactivity.

As we move into a more digital world with shorter attention spans and more content, we must make our campaigns more interactive. We need to step away from the broadcast e-mail trap of thinking that because we have sent an e-mail, we have communicated, and that our audience understands or is engaging with our message.

Communicators need to look at other disciplines such as gaming, learning and development, and training theories to be more interactive and add the gamification element that has an addictive element to keep people's attention. The ethical question right now is should we be using these techniques with our employees? I don't have an answer to this, but it is easy to look at the everyday marketing techniques being used around us and say that we are being far more moderate, because externally they do not have a duty of care to the people they are communicating with.

Our attention spans have shortened to the length of a Tweet (now known as an x on X by direction from Elon Musk, but this may have changed again). Our people multitask in online meetings.

I'm not sure about you, but unless your audience is actively participating, you can assume that you probably don't have their attention.

Attention is the biggest global commodity right now.

Technically, as Tim Wu, author of *The Attention Merchants* puts it, marketers, communicators, and advertisers are to blame:

> If the attention merchants were once primitive, one-person operations, the game of harvesting human attention and reselling it to advertisers has become a major part of our economy… Existing industries have long depended on it to drive sales. And the new industries of the twentieth century turned it into a form of currency they could mint.

What's more, learning by doing is a credible way of helping people understand and absorb your message. If your people are involved, they are paying attention. This is why so many change projects are coupled with learning and development programs run by the HR team in an organization.

Gamification is not a new concept. It takes interactivity to the next level and introduces competitiveness, goals, and a sense of accomplishment. The word "gamification" was accepted into the Oxford Dictionary in 2012. I particularly love this part of the definition:

"Gamification is exciting because it promises to make the hard stuff in life fun."

I see it as incorporating typical elements of game playing such as being actively involved with a specific goal or task, point scoring, competition with others, and problem or task solving.

But what do games have to do with communication? One of the goals of gamification is to influence behavior. If we go back to our industry model of multidirectional communication, brought to life through social media, we also see many gamification and interactive elements in social media communication. From an internal communication perspective, the question is are you directing your people's attention wisely and what value is being gained through gamifying an experience. I have seen incredible solutions cocreated through hackathons and also massive amounts of time and money spent on meaningless corporate games.

Appeal to the Senses

We have five senses. Some argue more, but why do we focus on written and video communication, completely ignoring our other senses?

Sound

Sound plays such an essential role in our communication. When I worked at SBS radio, Australia's multilingual and multicultural public broadcaster, early on in my career, I appreciated radio for its immediacy, and the ability to get into everyone's home and connect people with their community.

This is where I learned the value of communicating in one's native language and the celebration of different voices and accents. This is where I learned to appreciate what sound can bring to a story.

> The sound and the music are 50 percent of the entertainment in a movie.
>
> —George Lucas

It wasn't until later in my career that I realized that internal communicators don't use much audio. Shel Holtz and I discussed this in Ben's Deli, and we confirmed that we both only knew of a handful of case studies. For example, I'd heard that at Amazon, which hosts online stores in many countries, the associates who work in the warehouses helping the picking and packing process have a company radio. A DJ mixes music with prerecorded corporate messages broadcast through the warehouse. The staff can request songs and give feedback using an instant messaging app on their smartphone.

Sound is all around us, from birds chirping outside our window to our refrigerator's humming as we work from home. Films and movies use sound to create tension and excitement and convey emotion and nuances. We should be doing this in corporate communication too. Many marketing brands have already created their brand sounds.

Did you know that even the Berlin public transport system, Berliner Verkehrsbetriebe (BVG), has created a sound identity? Berlin is a city of 3.7 million people from over 190 countries. It has a reputation for being a diversity-rich capital with various lifestyles, cultures, and gender identities. The BVG aims to bring this diversity together by helping people on their journeys through the vibrant city. They created their sound design to reflect this by recording many voices and sounds in Berlin and blending them with the bass clarinet, the closest instrument to the human voice. They also chose a distinctive voice actress, Philippa Jarke, to embody the brand's sound. The BVG has a lovely brand identity and their sound identity adds richness. It is an area of marketing that I believe could add value to internal communication.

Touch

Touch can be incorporated into campaigns by using tactile components. Although digital first is ideal, something must be said about using tactile elements in communication campaigns. For example, with a fully virtual event, sometimes packages can be posted ahead of time with promotional things inside—a cap for everyone to wear for the meeting or playing cards for an activity. In our digital world, we often forget about the appeal of promotional items that used to be organized for staff as a part of a campaign.

Smell

Smell is interesting, as it is one of the first senses we become aware of as a child. As previously mentioned, for the Mykel Dixon event, a scent consultant curated the smells, to help us feel various emotions at different times (but I'm not sure if it worked). If we want to get fancy, olfactic communication is a nonverbal communication channel that refers to how humans and animals communicate and connect through their sense of smell. Keep in mind that different people perceive distinct smells in different ways. I had a lovely discussion with a dear friend and previous manager of mine, Abderazzaq Noor, who pointed out to me that some people experience smells like cardamom differently or could be hypersensitive to smells. There are also cultural elements that influence people's perceptions. Think of the smell of fresh bread wafting out of a bakery signaling that their products are hot out of the oven, or that fresh citrus smell released in an airplane when you are supposed to wake up. Scents can evoke memories and feelings and influence an experience.

Marketers have known about the power of smell for a long time, but from an internal communication perspective, we haven't really worked out how to use this knowledge. I would like to see us exploring these types of immersive communication in areas such as making the office experience more attractive and fostering employee well-being. While some offices have "chill out zones," I haven't yet heard of scents being used to enhance the message of relaxation in addition to all the plants and cushions you'll find in those zones. I have, however, heard of people who use scents for rituals such as starting or ending the workday, when working from home.

In contrast to the limited understanding of olfactory communication in internal communication, marketer, Marissa Sanfilippo says: "The science of scent marketing and scent branding has advanced to the point where companies can be very specific about the desired reaction. If the retailer is looking for a high-end appeal, the smell of leather is the way to go. Linen and cotton evoke cleanliness, good health, and springtime."

However, until the last few years, businesses couldn't widely apply olfactic techniques in the digital world as the technology wasn't available. This is changing as two branches of digital olfaction technology emerge: One focusing on digital detection and analysis of various odors, and the other focusing on digital transmission and re-creation of smells. There are start-ups in Europe and America working in this space, with a solid link to machine learning and AI in developing the technology. For example, at the National University of Singapore, researchers have been working with both smell and taste digital simulation. Associate Professor Yen Ching-Chiuan, the codirector of the NUS CUTE Center and from the NUS College of Design and Engineering in Singapore, and his team have been working with multisensory suits for traffic accident and hazmat emergency responder training.

In addition to VR sight and sound, the suits can replicate the sense of heat and the smell of smoke. In early August 2023, Yen told me that their technology was close to commercialization but had been delayed due to Covid-19. One of the University of Singapore's multisensory games, The Lost Foxfire, debuted in 2019.

The setup for "The Lost Foxfire" game system is entirely portable, so it can be put up in any room. The additional sensory cues in the form of heat and smell create a more immersive gameplay environment for the players, something rarely seen in current games.

—Associate Professor Yen Ching-Chiuan, Codirector of the Keio-NUS CUTE Center, supervisor of the project

Taste

Taste is also a sense to consider, and like smell, is still more restricted to in-person events. This is why food selection at conferences and events is so important. For employee events, the quality, selection, and taste of the food provided are often used as a signal to the employees of their worth.

As you'll read in the case study with Betina Sørensen, I've worked on hybrid events where taste was incorporated to add to the experience. For example, for one Covid-19 era online event, all remote participants for a European and United Kingdom industrial supply company leadership summit were asked to buy specific chocolate and chip products produced by their customers, and these items were incorporated into the event to add to the togetherness experience.

When I asked Yen about the future of digital tastes, he said it was still a work in progress. Interestingly, they could not produce sweet tastes based on their current technology. From a mass communication perspective, he felt their research had been beneficial as they had integrated their multisensory approach into game simulation and training, which had all produced good outcomes. It still looks quite uncomfortable and invasive from the photos of the current digital taste simulation from the University of Singapore's research. Try to visualize a large clear box that you hold with two hands to your mouth. The box is filled with wires and electronics. Two prongs stick out and touch your tongue and this is how you experience the digital taste. We'll see more developments in this space shortly.

Engaging More Richly With Your Audience

By deliberately considering and engaging your target audience with as many senses as possible, you'll not only increase your chance of communication connecting with an individual's preferences but also provide a more immersive experience.

We've covered understanding your stakeholder group and target audience in the section about foundational internal communication. To be effective with immersive communication, we need to move to the next level of understanding of your audiences. Particularly in an age of AI, with so much content noise around us, the skill is in the personalization and audience-centric view.

Design thinking principles are also now used for designing communication experiences. Developed at Stanford University in 2004 by David Kelly and Bernard Roth, this human-centric approach to problem-solving is now also being taught at universities such as RMIT University in Melbourne in the field of communication. I've also seen it used in best practice employee technology projects as a way to understand human needs, define the problem, ideate, prototype, and then test and refine the ideas. This methodology of in-depth research and idea refinement is also very useful for strategic alignment throughout the organization, because it creates a shared understanding of the benefits of involving different stakeholder groups in working through the problem definition and process.

Questions to Ask to See If a More Immersive Strategy Is Needed

- Is this a more complex campaign where you want to appeal to your audience on a more fundamental, experience-based level?
- What technologies are or could be available for scalability?
- What technical limitations (such as Internet speed) would the team need to consider?
- What is your budget for the outcome you want?

Case Study: Doing It Tandem Style

One of my favorite campaigns was for a global engineering company, who wanted to bring their technology team closer to an IT agency they'd started working with. This was on the Covid-19 tail at the end of 2021 and they wanted a global event, a two-day summit. The purpose was connection and collaboration to set them up for working well together in the future. We were all burned out on Zoom meetings, but meeting in person was not a solid option. Flights were expensive. Rules were still in place, and it was simply not possible. So, it became a virtual festival. An internal communication consultancy that I was working with was on board to do the concept and employee communication. Somewhere along the line, a hot pink flamingo with a 1980s Miami Vice sunset-style background ended up as the key image. A playlist was born to give more of a multisensory, interactive element. But the full campaign wasn't gelling. It was still a collection of ideas.

The Danish concept developer from the consultancy, Betina Sørensen, who is an outside-of-the-box thinker, was called into the project team to help. The team had gotten stuck and they'd come to her to bring in a fresh perspective and help the whole concept and narrative make sense.

"Every time I try to go into a creative process, I need to be clear on the problem that I'm trying to solve," Betina explained in her soft, husky voice as we sat down over coffee.

> I'm not talking about the overall purpose of an initiative, but trying to get down to the core, and being clear on what I'm trying to achieve with a creative approach, idea, or concept at the level of a single human being. For instance, the problem could be what kind of emotion or understanding that we're trying to spark in people's heads.
>
> Creative ideas are born in all kinds of ways. Sometimes it starts with something, a spontaneous idea, you fall in love with, sometimes it is more of a deliberate thought process. In this case, the core problem that needed solving was to make people from two different companies feel like one team and this wasn't yet present in the elements, it was still a lot of fun festival concepts.

Betina sees four stages in the creative process. The first one is Investigation, where you research things such as terminologies, what the audience is interested in, the images in their heads, and the culture of that specific group. It is a universe of visuals and words.

"Somewhere along the way with the universe of a music festival in place, we had the phrase "rocking IT," which can also be read as "rocking it," and in my head, I started hearing music and song lyrics," Betina explained.

The second stage is Ideation. This is where Betina considers what could be interesting, and what directions she could take the idea in. From there she looks at Conceptualization.

"In a brainstorm around 'Two is better than one', 'Oppa Gangnam Style' from the Korean PSY hit song, popped into my head, and a connection was made. This became Rocking IT tandem style," said Betina with a humble smile, peeking over her glasses. "We ended up with two flamingos on a tandem bike, with the front of the bike in the company's blue color with logos and the back in the IT consultancy's purple."

"Using the tandem bike as a symbol of people doing things together and relying on each other to get where they want to go," said Betina.

Lastly comes Implementation. This is where all the deliverables—what is produced to be shared—come out. Things such as a video, info screen, Microsoft Teams background, or e-mail. Words and visuals need to be tweaked for each deliverable to make sure they all fit together in the bigger picture. From my experience to date, AI can be used for ideation, making words crisper or mashing pictures, but ultimately the artist is the human at the helm who understands the meaning and needs to guide the technology to produce what is needed.

The concept of "Rocking IT tandem style" was applied by the internal communication consultancy across all of the deliverables, meeting budget needs. For example, the team used existing dancing flamingo GIFs to save budget and just added conceptual copy. The success was in the details of how the concept was applied, the fun opening video, and the coming together of play, dance, music, and people. Physical props were also planned, and there was a food element and festival wristbands. A playlist. It was multisensory.

Betina is someone who is always bursting with color, and always on the go. When I asked how she knew when the concept and the deliverables were right, she paused.

"It just feels right," Betina said. "It's when it's intuitive and simple to people. When you show it to them you don't need to explain a lot."

In the end, the event brought over 400 colleagues together across 40 countries and 30 nationalities. Business-standard technology was used to create a more immersive experience without actually using immersive technology. This included Microsoft Teams (video conferencing and collaboration), Spotify, (music streaming service), and Slido, (which allows for live display of interactive polling). Throughout the online event, every activity, presentation, and session appealed to the senses and engaged the audience. Many of the sessions throughout the festival deliberately had interactive, gamified elements.

Most importantly, like the Rethink cartoon campaign from chapter four, the people took on the initiative as their own.

"They really embraced it," Betina said. "After the event, we heard there had been friendly banter, such as apologizing for noisy flamingos in the background." The investment was recognized as being valuable in bringing the teams together, and another "flamazing" IT fest was held the following year.

"These days we can get so afraid of stepping outside the lines, that we risk that no one sees the coloring inside the lines," Betina said. "So, I kind of want to color a little bit at the edge and sometimes just a little outside the lines to trigger an emotion and actual change in people's minds.

Betina's tips on bringing creativity to organizations are as follows:

- Remember that organizations are also just people, so always focus on the people.
- Recognize that ideas come from curiosity. Open your eyes, listen, and encourage others to be curious.
- Give time for ideas to percolate. Allow creative people to step away and let their brains relax; that's when the ideas or the creative connection will happen.

Be bold and aim to push the boundaries—this can be in a tone of voice, or by provoking people to think.

ACTIVITY—*Review Your Internal Communication Habits*

Critically look at the last communication project that you were involved in. How many senses did it appeal to?

- Were all the videos talking head videos?
- Was most of the communication text-based?
- What senses did the campaign appeal to?

- Did the communication have a rigid structure, or were the people who might have been away on vacation still able to understand the following messages and information without having missed a key concept?
- Was there a chance for people to be involved? Cocreate? Actively learn by doing?

Once you have a clear picture of the typical implementation plans your organization runs, challenge yourself to think about how the experience could be more immersive for the audience.

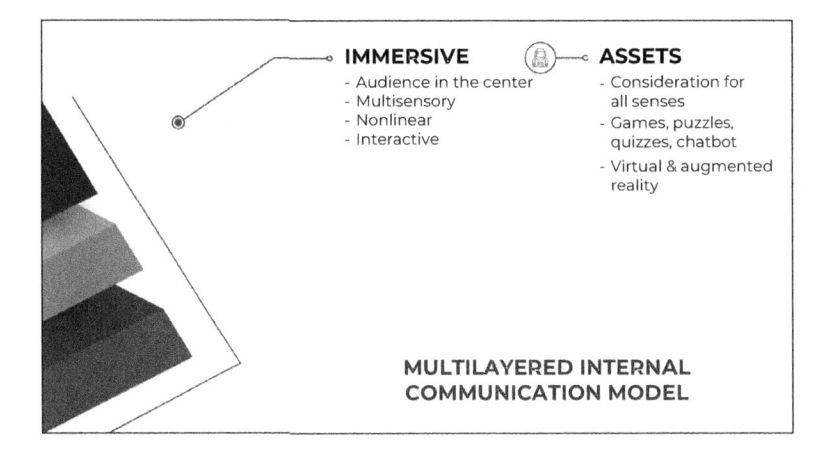

IMMERSIVE
- Audience in the center
- Multisensory
- Nonlinear
- Interactive

ASSETS
- Consideration for all senses
- Games, puzzles, quizzes, chatbot
- Virtual & augmented reality

MULTILAYERED INTERNAL COMMUNICATION MODEL

Key Takeaways

Immersive communication techniques reduce the friction between sender and receiver and puts the audience in the center of the experience. It is more persuasive and ideal for more complex campaigns.

- Often there is no need for technology; immersive communication is a mindset. Immersive communication should be nonlinear, multidirectional, and interactive.
- As kids, we learn through play. For adults it's equally effective.
- Immersive communication involves the blending of communication, engagement, and learning.
- Technological developments, including in the areas of AI, will improve scalability of communication in the future.

CHAPTER 6

Leadership Communication

What You Say and Do and What Others Say About You

We could hear yelling. Loud. The head of our public relations company in Washington, DC, was giving one of our lead communication advisers a piece of her mind, and we could all hear. The door was shut to her office, one of the two box-like flimsy offices on either side of the enormous window that looked out over the capital from Georgetown.

The lead communication adviser Pam quietly opened the door and came out. We all pretended that we hadn't heard or weren't paying attention. I can't remember if she silently sat at her desk or walked past us out of the building. Either way, with her elegantly bobbed blond hair and stern face, she was respected for her skills and previous experience as a spokesperson for a large pharmaceutical company. Experienced and tough. But, in that split moment, as she stepped out of the office, we saw the pain and shame in her eyes. The door made a hollow rattle as she clicked it shut behind her.

Trust and Authenticity

As a leader, as a person, what you say and do, and what others say about you builds your trust value. These three things need to align. If there is a misalignment, it erodes the trust people have in you.

We had been told that we were valued employees at the public relations agency, but we could see that public humiliation was okay.

Some could argue that what the head of the company had been doing was being authentic and expressing her frustrations to Pam.

I know that authenticity is admired in a leader, but as Seth Godin points out, it is overrated. I used to be a huge advocate of authentic leadership

TRUST TRIANGLE

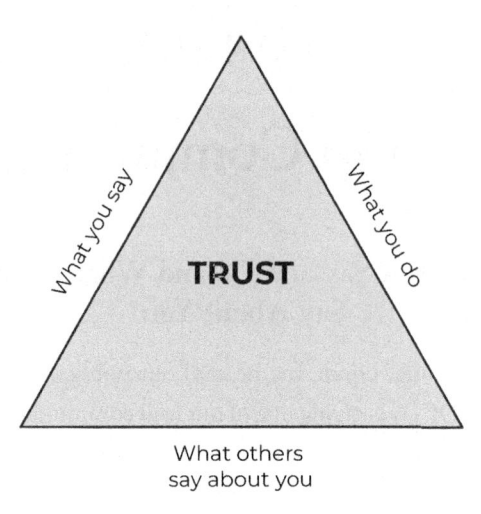

What you say / *What you do*

TRUST

What others
say about you

until I heard one of Seth's podcasts on this some years ago and gave it some serious thought. I found an online YouTube video, *Seth Godin: Authenticity Is Overrated. Here's What You Need Instead*, that explains it well. Here is an extract of his rant that beautifully gets to the point.

> Authenticity is overrated ... Because the last time you were authentic, you were three months old, laying in diapers ... Ever since then, you have done things with intent. You have done things on purpose. You wake up in the morning, and you don't feel like going to work; you go to work. If we hire a professional to do surgery on our knee or paint our house, we don't want them to show up and say I had a fight with my spouse, and I'm going to do a lousy job today. That would be authentic, but not what we want.
> —Seth Godin

It is the role of the communicator to work with their leaders to help them shine in a human, relatable way, trustworthy, and consistent.

It doesn't matter if the communication expert is the chief of staff, head of public relations, or director of internal communication; managing the alignment between what a leader says, their actions, and how others talk about them is critical now, more than ever.

Leadership is intentional. It plays an important role in the communication landscape. A leader's trust value, reputation, and image can be managed through careful communication, planning to bring the most benefit to a company and its business goals. It also boosts reputation and standing, opening doors to new opportunities.

Just as a leader's reputation is managed externally, so should it be handled internally. Both need to align. The internal positioning is like an extra layer that relates specifically to what the employees in the company care about and can, if appropriate, be reflected externally on their personal social media platforms.

Suppose we delve a little deeper into the idea of trust and lean into the work of Brené Brown, research professor at the University of Houston in her book *Dare to Lead*. Building on Charles Feltman's definition, she states that "trust is the stacking and layering of small moments and reciprocal vulnerability over time. Trust and vulnerability grow together, and to betray one is to destroy both." Brené closely links trust building with vulnerability sharing. A skilled communication professional will be able to weave the right amount of vulnerability into the communication when crafting a leader's image, speeches, and e-mails. I always find it essential to talk with my clients about what they are comfortable sharing publicly and what is off-limits. It makes me contemplate if, when people talk about authenticity, they mean infusing vulnerability into their public profile.

I talk about public profiles because everything we do within an organization is shared. Technology has made this easier both in terms of proof sharing and amplification.

In March 2023, the CEO of office furniture giant MillerKnoll became an instant social media celebrity for the wrong reasons when she gave a live video town hall to employees telling them to "leave pity city" in response to their questions and concerns about their bonuses not being paid out.

The meeting was recorded by an employee and the video went viral through YouTube, LinkedIn, and several social media and mainstream media channels, followed by her written apology being smeared across digital media.

Why Does Leadership Trust and Communication Matter?

Returning to the idea of trust, Brené Brown also talks about how "trust is the glue that holds teams and organizations together. We ignore trust issues at the expense of our performance and our team's and organization's success."

Trust has a currency that will grow exponentially in the coming years as the external media environment around us continues to erode trust. The value of trust is not new. Many leaders and communication people across the globe wait with bated breath for the release of the annual Edelman Trust Barometer, which has grown in prominence over the last 20 years. Trust became particularly important as we all navigated the Covid-19 pandemic, unsure at the start of how the virus was transmitted or how we should exactly manage the spread. There was conflicting information, different decisions and approaches by other countries, and much polarization. This follows an extensive uncovering of opinion manipulation and election influencing by Cambridge Analytica through social media.

Disinformation can set the scene within which we now operate. And it's fueled by technology, which can slice and dice the distribution of content and tailor it to a specific person's content feed algorithm.

With AI, deep fakes are constantly getting better and less detectable. A deep fake is an image or recording that is computer generated through deep learning AI, which presents someone doing or saying something that was not done or said. One of the first deep fakes that grabbed worldwide attention was "In Event of Moon Disaster," developed by the MIT Center for Advanced Virtuality. As a public project designed to educate people on the dangers of deep fakes, the seven-minute video shows U.S. President Richard M. Nixon delivering the actual contingency speech written in 1969 for a scenario where the Apollo 11 crew didn't return from the moon. The film and art installation first premiered on November 22, 2019, won many awards, and since then has been rapidly eclipsed by even more advanced deep fakes.

This means that we can no longer trust the video or photos we see and will need to constantly go back to the source and ask ourselves if the source is trustworthy and if the information presented can be corroborated by other credible sources. Anyone with the technology and knowledge can, with relative ease, create a "pity-city" deep fake to scuttle the ambitions of any leader.

In a publicly released talk "The AI Dilemma," technology ethicist Tristan Harris from the Center of Humane Technology pointed out that 2023 is the year for reality collapse and trust collapse, building on his messages from his two-time Emmy award-winning film, *The Social Dilemma*. We can no longer tell what is true. We cannot believe what we see or hear. In early 2023, it was already possible to synthesize a voice with a three-second voice sample. Deep fakes are becoming harder and harder to spot.

This makes trust an even more valuable commodity in our increasingly untrustworthy communication environment.

Building your trust profile is an investment for your future. As we can see from the trust model, internal communication, what the leader says, and what others say about the leader play a considerable role.

A communication expert, who has earned the role of a trusted adviser, is also responsible for influencing what the leader does. This means helping them make the right decisions and providing uncomfortable feedback. A leader's head in the sand is dangerous to the company and those around them.

Transformational Leaders Need to Be Exceptional Communicators

Communicating your vision and bringing others on the journey with you are powerful leadership skills. As an effective leader, you become an asset to a project, with a clear voice and leadership strength to persuade and motivate employees to do what is needed.

Communication is a necessary skill for leaders to be successful, but they don't need to do it alone. More senior leaders can call upon their internal communications teams to support them with their at-scale communication projects, and more emerging leaders, with strategic nous, can do their own communication initiatives, with support from trusted colleagues or their executive assistant to give feedback along the way.

Communication is a skill that needs to be practiced and can be improved. Combined with strategic alignment and stakeholder management, it holds all of the communication layers together. This is visualized in the following multilayered internal communication model.

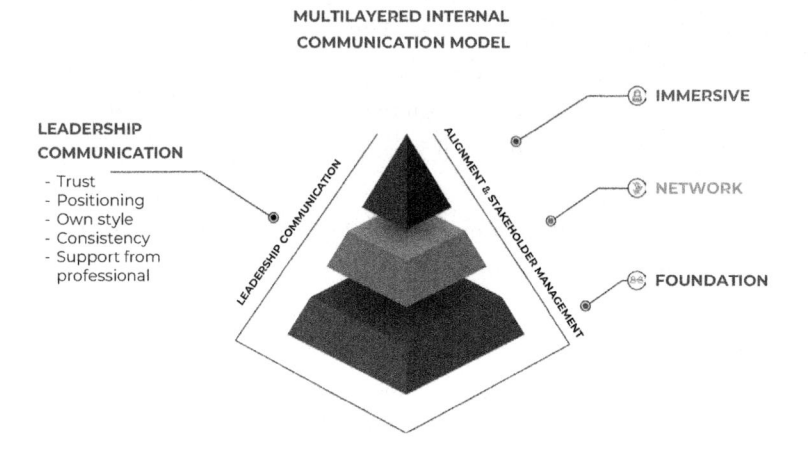

MULTILAYERED INTERNAL COMMUNICATION MODEL

LEADERSHIP COMMUNICATION
- Trust
- Positioning
- Own style
- Consistency
- Support from professional

- IMMERSIVE
- NETWORK
- FOUNDATION

Leadership communication involves not only how the leader wants to be positioned but also how it can benefit an internal communication campaign.

How to Get Leadership Communication Right

Because this book is about strategy, let's start with the big-picture strategy. We need to look at a leader's position, what they stand for, their values and vision, their communication strengths, and preferences. From here, all the communication flows.

Too often, I read general hints and tips on leadership communication, such as "be authentic and open" or "use storytelling," but this doesn't begin to scratch the surface of what effective leadership communication looks like. It isn't about broad brushstroke principles; it is about the leader strategizing with their communication experts on how to communicate to build trust, gather power, and be a sustainable, effective leader themselves. It is about creating a personal approach that works to the leader's strengths and downplays anything that isn't working. It is about growth for the leader as a communicator.

This is why it is important to spend time on the strategy to consistently apply it across all of your internal communications and ensure that it is reflected in external communication. I'd also recommend that you read up on personal branding, which is an art in itself. Jeff Bezos, the founder of Amazon, said, "Your brand is what people say when you are not in the room." Personal branding is a conscious and intentional effort to shape people's perception of you and build your reputation, as one would with a company. While it is a similar approach for both the individual and the organization, personal branding must be positioned with what is important within the workplace and for the people who work there, particularly the ones the leader wants to influence.

Case Study: Good Leadership Communication Can Be Learned

One of my internal communication friends in Tacoma, Washington, Daven Rosener, founder at Amplify IC, has a humble smile when he quietly tells the story of how one of his CEOs had initially, completely, and royally bombed when presenting to 500 managers. A star in the boardroom but extremely nervous in front of larger groups, the CEO had insisted on detailed slides to draw his audience's attention to the screen rather than looking at him and noticing what he was saying. As the eyes of most of the 500 managers had started to glaze over, the CEO, a big man, had rapidly skipped through the last of the slides, feeling the lack of interest in the room.

"The detailed, content-heavy slides signaled to the audience that they needed to read every slide. They were reading," says Daven. "Yes, they were very interested in the slides, but they wanted their leader more."

Daven paused and smiled as he remembered. He went on and explained that no one had expected the CEO to be a perfect presenter.

For the next presentation, Daven worked with his CEO to craft a story focusing on what the CEO was passionate about, allowing him to play to his strengths and deliver the right speech.

> This time, the audience was mesmerized when the CEO spoke genuinely about his pride in them. He choked up, became emotional, and had tears in his eyes. Showing emotion helped the audience connect with him. His people listened.
>
> This is a perfect example of how a leader can learn to be a more engaging communicator. It is also a great example of an internal communication professional helping the leader shine and try a new approach that got results.

Get a Good Communication Professional

An experienced communication professional should be curious, ask many questions, and ensure communication aligns with business strategy. They will try to get to the bottom of your business problems and show how your leadership and strategic communication can help solve organizational issues. They are not your promotion machine, so if you are a leader and they willingly take orders without questioning you, get someone more senior.

Leadership Positioning

Work out what you stand for with three to five key issues aligned with the organization. What you talk about should revolve around these topic pillars.

Skilled internal communicators will look at the senior leaders and ensure that each profile supports the rest and that the leadership team looks like it is pulling its weight. Nothing is worse than focusing only on the head of the company, instead of the whole leadership team, and then losing all of that leadership positioning work both internally and externally as the leader finishes their tenure.

One leader may focus on a specific area of diversity and inclusion and another on innovation. All need to be aligned with the overall corporate strategy and company positioning.

What Are Your Leadership Communication Strengths?

Play to your strengths. It is what will make you stand out and succeed. Some leaders are great in a small group setting; they quickly have their people hanging onto every word as the leader does a floor walk. Other leaders naturally excel at the big town hall event. As part of getting to know their leader, an internal communication professional needs to discover their leader's strengths, challenge them on assumptions, and give feedback along the way.

Having stood on world stages and presented, I know how nerve-wracking that can feel. Regardless of how well you have practiced, transforming those butterflies into energy and calming the heart rate as it naturally accelerates in anticipation is challenging.

Understanding your communication strengths and being able to consciously create environments where you will excel makes sense. Deliberately use your own style that matches your brand.

The Leader's Vantage Point

One of Australia's top speechwriters, Lucinda Holdforth, is not only a lovely, well-spoken, and humble speechwriter but also a university lecturer and author of several books including *Leading Lines: How to Make Speeches That Seize the Moment, Advance Your Cause and Lead the Way*. She beautifully explains the impact and power of a strategically crafted speech. She shows how the leader wants to be perceived by a specific audience and how that knowledge influences how a speech is written and put together. One thing that communicators often miss is carefully selecting the vantage point for each piece of communication. A gut feeling usually takes over, or the savvy leader has a sense, but as with all things strategic, nailing it down and making a deliberate decision is essential.

The vantage point is where the leader is standing, both in terms of perspective (bird's eye view or close to an issue) and point in time. It is influenced by whom they are communicating with and where they are communicating from.

For example, a speech from the United Nations, standing among the world's leaders in a critical moment in history should be different from how a leader would position themselves to show they understand popular culture.

Let's take Michelle Obama's carpool karaoke in 2016 with *The Late Show*'s James Corden where the First Lady enthusiastically sings and grooves to Beyoncé in the car with James Corden driving. Compare this to her 2016 speech on International Women's Day in Washington, DC, where she spoke about fighting for women's rights. Both are with a smile and charm, but from very different viewpoints that fit with different messages.

While many leaders that I've worked with have a sense of how they want to position themselves, it can often be helpful to think about how each piece of communication, and by that, I mean each tactic, such as an all-staff e-mail or speech, needs to shift slightly based on the vantage point and how it is relevant to that moment in time.

Your Origin Story

OK, so yes, let's use storytelling. Your origin story is the story you tell to explain why you believe something. It is about what shaped you as a leader. In my case, I tell the story of how I was a physiotherapist and realized that I could identify the day my patient wanted to get better, and then they would. My role as a physiotherapist was largely about understanding the person and helping them take ownership of their recovery. This is how I became interested in persuasion, motivation, and all the dark arts of communication.

Your origin story needs to shift and change as you grow as a leader and must align with your leadership positioning within your organization at that moment. It needs to contribute to your trust profile and personal brand.

Storytelling

Let's zoom out here and look at storytelling more broadly. It is a powerful tool that many communicators use to help make a point, bring facts to life, or make a topic relatable to others. But, like all tools in your toolbox, it shouldn't be used all the time. There is nothing more annoying than a leader launching into a story when you have the feeling that they are just trying to sell you bad news.

The stories need to be relevant and told well. They need to be short and to the point. They should also demonstrate your values and show who you are.

Many leaders I know test stories on different audiences, usually starting with one or two people, to see how the story lands. They also play with timing, what emphasis is given to different parts of the story, and even body language to try and make the right impact. I've also consulted with leaders on the types of metaphors that suit their brand and story so they can confidently lean on them during storytelling. People I know have done stand-up comedy courses and even hired actors to help them learn better ways of delivering their messages. There are plenty of great books, YouTube videos, and online articles to help you delve deeper into the art of influential storytelling. Look up Gabrielle Dolan, Daniel Kahneman, Yuval Noah Harari, and Rob Biesenbach, to name a few.

Consistency

Now, more than ever, people crave consistency. With all of the change swirling around us, reliability is valued.

By planning out regular communication touch points and their formats with your people, you are giving them assurance that you will communicate with them and make yourself available to them. By this, I mean looking at each group of employees you want to communicate with, knowing your communication strengths, planning regular meetings, tours, and visits, and working out the right mix for your situation.

Try to prioritize these techniques; canceling meetings or other commitments without clear reasons signals to your people that you do not value them.

But consistency doesn't mean boring.

Each opportunity to communicate should be well-thought-out and positioned. Harness your team to take turns hosting the branch meeting, where the key leader is the star, and share ownership.

Good Communicators Hold More Sustainable Power

As an intern in the agency back in Washington, DC, in our open-plan office with our view over the city, we formed a supportive bond with the interns (us) versus them, the permanent employees. I learned all types of strategies to negate poor leadership communication.

Let me tell you about the elephant strategy. I learned this from one of the other interns who let me in on the secret. The idea was to deliberately include a significant error or mistake in our work. We'd call it the elephant in the room because it was apparent. It was big. It was obvious. We had learned that no matter how good the work we did, there was always some sort of picking feedback, and we discovered that if we put a major mistake in the document, this would be picked up and the rest of the document left alone. A lot less revision work for us. This reactive strategy is what can happen when trust and communication break down.

Imagine if there had been a culture of trust and nurturing. Imagine if we had been respected.

A part of being human is to make mistakes. We all do. With a bank full of trust within your organization and being seen as a leader who generally does the right thing, when mistakes are made, more leeway is given, especially when the leader owns their mistake and takes responsibility.

Going "Glocal"

"About 50 percent of my job is communication and about 80 percent of the time when things go wrong it is because of bad communication in a project, between teams or something else," confessed a senior vice president of DB Schenker to me over a delicious Thai mango curry lunch. "Communication is such an important part of my role."

In such a global role, in addition to leadership communication, intercountry communication was at the forefront of his mind. How do you communicate between different teams in different locations, to not only get clear messages through to your people but also help them work together across cultures and languages?

Glocal is when you have a global focus but go local with your interpretation and messaging. For something like this to be sustainable, set up a community structure that will allow for information to flow in all directions, not just from central to spoke, like in a hub-and-spoke organizational structure. Always invest in having someone in the local culture check your messaging and consult with them on any sensitivities.

Always start by listening. What do the employees in that country or office need? What questions do they have? What is confusing them?

Scan to listen

IABC EMENA podcast. "Localising global communication with Ray Walsh and Cecilia Maldonado," December 13, 2021.
https://on.soundcloud.com/Bwjyx

Questions to Ask Yourself as a Leader, as a Communicator

- What is my brand and how do others see me?
- Do my actions match my words?
- What are my three topic pillars, and how are the other leaders around me positioned?
- What do the people around me want and need to see in a leader right now?
- How might I need to transition this perception in the future?
- Am I using a range of feedback methods to inform my opinion?
- Am I communicating consistently? Remember, this doesn't mean always sharing; this means communicating consistently.

The three key elements to focus on are a clear position on what you stand for, building trust, and ensuring consistent communication. This makes leadership communication much more effective.

Case Study: Embracing Sound in Leadership Communication

I first met Bhanu Prakash in 2021 when I interviewed him for a podcast. Calling in from Dubai while I was in Berlin, I enjoyed his passion for internal communication and how his brain worked. It wasn't until after we'd stopped recording that we got to talk about how he had set up a corporate radio for Amazon employees working in the warehouse. We'd had to be a bit careful at the time about what we'd discussed in the podcast, so this one was off-air. I loved this idea of using the more informal corporate communications that a radio offers, particularly for people picking and packing, that didn't demand that the employees read anything. Bhanu said the staff loved it. "They could use a particular WhatsApp number to request songs or dedicate a song or message to different employees," Bhanu explained. "Our associates could also send recorded messages and give feedback to the DJ, and the best part was they were able to share feedback on specific campaigns as well."

The corporate messages along with music had been prerecorded and then scheduled the day before. The radio content could also be easily changed if needed because radio is such an immediate communication method. I remember the immediacy of radio in getting out to the people when working at SBS Radio, that is, the ability to quickly switch direction with a broadcast if fresh news landed, giving that sense of happening in real time.

More recently, Bhanu and I caught up, and he shared a lovely case study highlighting how simple and effective well-thought-through leadership communications can be. When he was the head of internal communication for Amazon's Middle East and North Africa region's operations, he realized that the head of operations had very few touchpoints with his employees. There was only a biannual town hall along with site visits. There were not many opportunities for the leader to be visible or communicate effectively with their teams. While e-mails can be a quick fix but are a bit uninspiring, and videos are expensive to do right, Bhanu, with his keen ears, came up with another idea.

"We wanted to bring emotion and connect with employees," Bhanu explained. "So I sat with the leader and conceptualized a way to bring his voice to the people."

They started with a few podcasts covering what was on the leader's mind, focusing on the usual topics of the day. As the regional head of operations became comfortable and started seeing the benefits, he quickly shifted to wanting to interview other senior leaders.

This is what sparked my interest because it signals a shift in leadership positioning toward a more collaborative personal brand.

The head of operations started by interviewing Ronaldo Mouchawar (Ronnie), CEO and founder of Souq, which was initially the largest e-commerce platform in the Arab world and was acquired by Amazon in 2017. From here, more and more leaders across Amazon were invited to be interviewed, discussing topics such as how the different leaders and their teams could work better together. This allowed for genuine discussions that were relevant to the employees.

"It helped in two ways, by building relationships and by positioning himself as a credible leader in other regions," Bhanu explained. "His podcast was going worldwide to different staff members and talked about our region's success factors."

"Because it had a really personal tone and was in his voice, people felt they could reach out to him," Bhanu said. "It significantly improved people's awareness and perception of him as a leader. And employees could also share the topics they wanted to hear from their leader." In this way, although radio is technically one-directional, a broadcast medium, feedback mechanisms were put in place to shift it toward dialogue and allow for organizational listening.

The podcasts were, on average, 12 to 15 minutes long, had an average of 35 percent listenership, and were the first of its kind in Amazon Internal Communication worldwide. Putting this into the context of an average 10 to 12 percent listenership for internal communications, and intranet stories getting 10 percent readership, these results are outstanding.

Scan to listen

IABC EMENA podcast. "Bhanu Prakash on cutting the clutter" May 25, 2021.
https://on.soundcloud.com/U4CxtBDikuZjNcFz5

Key Takeaways

Effectively communicating at scale is a powerful tool for business leaders to harness. If done well, it gives both business project and personal career benefits.

- Trust will continue to be one of the biggest leadership commodities.
- What you say, do, and others say about you needs to align to build and maintain trust.
- Be clear on your leadership communication style and personal brand in the company.
- Use storytelling wisely, including your origin story.
- Be consistent and communicate deliberately.
- Your internal communication expert is there to support you, challenge you, and help you communicate effectively across your organization.

CHAPTER 7

Strategic Alignment and Activating Your Team

Let's Align on That!

We stood in the schoolyard, clutching half-filled coffee cups that added warmth to our hands, looking at the queue of parents lining up at the coffee cart waiting to order. Each one was chatting to others in the queue, all with mismatched empty coffee mugs in their hands, cups that had been lent to them from the staff room so disposable cups didn't need to be used. The smell of the grinding coffee and the loud humming of the large espresso machine were both relaxing and exciting. The kids were already in class with their teachers, and we were all dawdling, chatting, and connecting before we headed to work from home or arrived a little late at work. The school community was coming back together, and something as simple as an invitation to stay after drop-off and a coffee truck parked on the school grounds brought us back into conversation and a sense of connectedness. I gave heartfelt thanks to the new school principal, who understood that communities don't just come together; there needs to be a reason. If coffee had been the reason, then it was fine by me.

One of the parents, Daniel, and I had been talking about what part of communicating at scale was most important to him as a leader. I'm always interested in what others think, and as a manager in a large, well-known American tech company, I was curious as to what challenges he was having leading his team.

Daniel scrunched up his face and peeked up at the clouds. One word popped out, "alignment." He looked at me. "Getting my team to align with what our company is doing," he said. "They have great ideas; we innovate well." But, prioritizing and spending time on what needed to be done within the teams was a lot of hard work for Daniel and his leadership group. He wanted to know how he could help his broader team (the branch) align with the bigger picture so they could better self-prioritize their projects and feel more involved.

I asked if his team members had skin in the game, and we talked a bit about that. Skin in the game is when you have an active interest in something, for example, when individual team members are put in the spotlight and need to step up and take responsibility for the outcome. If they don't put in the effort, it would reflect poorly on them as a person. Their reputation is on the line, they have skin in the game. Nowhere to hide for your efforts or decisions.

It is a strategy that I learned when working in a bar. My manager at the time, Torsten, in his 26-year-old wisdom, had given each of us specific responsibilities to deliver to the team. He let us make mistakes but was always there as a safety net to catch us before we metaphorically hit the floor. One of the bar staff members was in charge of deliveries and orders; I was in charge of the small cocktail bar on the side of the pub. None of us had any level of hierarchy above each other or the ability to have people reporting to us. Still, we certainly quickly understood how these different tasks contributed to how busy the bar was, how much customers spent, and ultimately, the evening receipts.

This is a great example of how Torsten led the what and why and trusted and empowered the team on the how. Micromanagement, which is very disempowering and absolves some responsibility, happens when the leader dictates the how.

Skin in the game was me reporting back to the rest of our group after closing and having cleaned up and counted the tills, whether we'd had a good night in the cocktail bar on the side of the pub. I hadn't been told when to start work, just when the bar needed to open. I hadn't been told how to arrange the furniture; that was up to me. Over time, I learned that customers were happy to buy more expensive drinks if we added flair or custom-created drinks based on what I knew they liked. If we got swamped, it was also up to me to ask for help from my manager or more staff members. But I also knew Torsten would pop around and check on me to make sure everything was going well. I often didn't notice him wandering past or his head poking through the door as his supervision was unintrusive. I knew, we all knew, that plenty of happy customers and a good night's return was what mattered. It meant more hours (and money) for us and more team members if we were consistently busy. We were paid on an hourly rate and our success at the bar would also be reflected in our tips, which we shared. We understood our goals and could make the connection between our decisions and reaching our goals. Because we felt valued, we were also motivated and engaged to follow through on what we knew would get results.

The story about when the refrigerator thermostat broke and how we helped Torsten drink all the frozen (and therefore unsellable) beverages, can be saved for another day.

What Exactly Is Strategic Alignment?

Strategic alignment refers to the extent to which people in the organization understand the company's goals and connect their daily work decisions to them. Gartner's research shows that this is the most crucial factor in driving high-performing teams.

In the age of AI, alignment is also a broader question, with the general consensus that AI should be aligned with human values and follow human intent. "Unaligned artificial general intelligence could pose substantial risks to humanity," says Leike et al. (2022) on the OpenAI website.

But the topic of AI is a broad one, and for example, because GenAI is trainable and can be customized to organizations, I see the opportunity for it to play a role in helping employees check if their ideas align with corporate strategy and conveniently write them a business case for their ideas. These concepts become important when we look at working with AI and technology, as well as the potential that it could offer in helping us with our humans aligning, but more of this later. Let's start with the people.

A good friend of mine, Zora Artis, a leading alignment, brand, and communication strategist, coauthored the global-first study on strategic alignment and the role of communicators and leadership. I interviewed her for a podcast to discuss organizational, leadership, and team strategic alignment. Originally from a Yugoslavian (Serbian) background, Zora is an impressive and confident communicator, familiar with working with global C-suite executives, and bold in calling things as they are.

She'd been working with a global corporate client to help their global leadership team develop their communication and alignment capability. This would help shift them from being good to great communicators. The focus was on assisting them to connect the dots between what they do on a day-to-day basis and what their teams do and connect that directly to their corporate strategy, their values, and how they work together across 30 countries.

Like any strategy, it is about understanding the baseline and current state. Zora starts with the exploratory phase, with stakeholder interviews, corporate and divisional strategies, and understanding the context. She does this with the company's internal communication team and a pilot team of global leaders to make sure they are on board. Zora also works with them to develop a strategic narrative, a one-pager cheat sheet, and a communication toolkit. Then a series of workshops and hands-on training help the leaders come to a common understanding, shifting their mindset, and lifting their capability. The aim is to get information out of people and to come to a common understanding of the situation and what needs to be done.

Alignment is important not only at the team, project, or function level but also alignment at a leadership and management level to help create a shared understanding across all layers of your organization. That's a lot of alignment. It does need work. It's why the team days or strategy days are important. In our digital world and for many companies, the experience needs to be rethought so that we continue to work on shared understanding rather than fragmented discussions punctuated by online calls, e-mail distractions, and other tasks popping up and grabbing our valuable attention.

Why are we talking about strategic alignment in a book about internal communication?

With newfound enthusiasm for communicating at scale within organizations, fancy technology, new platforms, and much talk about employee engagement, it is easy to lose sight of why organizations pay money for someone to do this job and why there are experts in this field. As Steffen Henke from DHL Group was cited in an earlier chapter, it is about corporate communication. It is about remembering that we are all focused on achieving our business goals.

Zora and I agree that a great employee experience leads to a better customer experience. A good employee experience will help you keep good employees and help them stay engaged with your organization, giving more discretionary effort. You might even have a high-performing team, that can be innovative, like Daniel's team, but unless they are kicking the right goals, your business won't go in the direction you want it to. A 2019 Garner research report showed that although 74 percent of managers had a solid commitment to the corporate strategy, they struggled with understanding how the strategy related to their team's function and their own job, significantly impacting the execution of strategy. So this isn't limited only to Daniel's management team, or organizations that I have worked with.

Zora articulated this beautifully by saying:

> You can have passionate people who are committed, engaged, and happy at work. But, if they're not aligned to what the organization needs, if they're not all heading in the same direction, with shared clarity and purpose, then they might be what you'd call free-range employees—working in silos. So, I think that if you look at how you combine employee engagement with experience and alignment, then you are more likely to have a high-performing, healthy organization—an organization that delivers on its promise not just to its customers but to its people as well.

Scan to listen

IABC EMENA podcast. "Organizational, leadership and team alignment with Zora Artis," June 6, 2022. https://on.soundcloud.com/TPqv2

Communication is excellent. Communicating at scale is great, but if employees don't have a shared understanding of where the organization needs to go and how to get there and skin in the game, then you can have productive, happy employees who are working in different directions and not toward a shared understanding of a common goal.

The purpose of alignment is so that your people can make the right decisions to support your business goals. It is about empowering your people, not micro-managing them. Daniel doesn't want to have to tell every single person in his extended team what to do. He wants them to use their judgment and understanding to make decisions that will contribute to the whole organization moving in the right direction. He also wants them to feel motivated to exercise their judgment.

The Relationship Between Alignment, Employee Experience, and Employee Engagement

Belinda Gannaway and I can't remember how we met, but we always have great conversations. We think we met through her research into organizational values, but we can't be sure. Belinda and I have so many people in common that it is embarrassing. She is a culture activation strategist, coach, and facilitator, based in Brighton in the United Kingdom. Her ideal holiday is sailing with someone who is a competent sailor, combined with lots of swimming. I guess it's a good thing that Great Britain (like Australia) is an island. Plenty of sea. She has sailed across the Atlantic but describes herself as a consciously incompetent sailor. Fortunately, Belinda is an expert in culture and employee experience. She is also coauthor, with Emma Bridger, of *Employee Experience by Design—How to Create an Effective EX for Competitive Advantage*.

Over one of our video calls, Belinda and I chatted about the relationship between strategic alignment, employee experience, and employee engagement. She describes it as being cyclical, where strategic alignment feeds into a great employee experience, which improves employee engagement and, in turn, fuels the employee's desire to participate in strategic alignment.

RELATIONSHIP BETWEEN EMPLOYEE ALIGNMENT, EXPERIENCE & ENGAGEMENT

Employee strategic alignment → Employee experience → Employee engagement → (cycle continues)

Organizational performance and success

Strategic alignment is critical for organizational performance and success. But it's also possible to look at this in another way, to consider how alignment and connection to the organization's purpose, mission, and strategy contribute to employee experience.

This model shows the relationship between employee alignment, experience, and engagement.

Belinda suggests that this is a significant, but often overlooked part of the alignment and performance equation.

- **Employee experience** is how employees feel about their experience across all elements of their interactions with the organization, its people, and the work. It is often looked at in terms of employee life cycle moments, such as onboarding, or career progression. While these are significant parts of employee experience, it is actually much broader and deeper than just these set-pieces.
- **Employee engagement** is the level of commitment, enthusiasm, and dedication that employees have toward their work and the organization. Engagement is largely a result of the experience employees have. Engagement is a product of employee experience.
- **Employee alignment** describes the understanding and acceptance employees have of the company's goals, purpose, mission, and strategy, AND the extent employees translate their understanding into action on a daily basis, for example how they make decisions and go about their work.

Although Belinda comes from an HR specialist viewpoint and I come from an internal communication perspective, both she and I are looking at the same diamond, but from different angles.

I see people ultimately being self-motivated. Behavioral change is about looking at how you can help align their motivation and understanding with the desired outcome—the company goals. This is no different from my time working as a physiotherapist, realizing that what was key to success was my understanding of what would motivate my patient or client to do their exercises. Sometimes, for an athlete, it was about what would inspire them to stop and rest. The patient needed to take responsibility for their own progress and the successful therapist would be able to work out how to influence this. For example, sometimes linking the activity with a habit such as brushing teeth and breaking it down into a manageable task was the solution, for others, giving them a clear vision of what they were working toward was necessary. Sometimes just listening and helping them feel heard was the answer.

Belinda explained it from a business perspective.

> For that knowledge to convert into behavior, there needs to be a catalyst. Employees need to identify with the company and what it stands for, care about it, and feel a sense of connection and belonging. That identification, care, and connection are both a requirement of a great employee experience and a result of it. But they don't happen by accident. To achieve both parts of true alignment—knowledge and action—it's vital to also work on employee experience. That means starting with an understanding of the people you have in the organization, rather than a list of predetermined assumptions, and designing an experience that addresses their unique needs, expectations, and motivations.
>
> —Belinda Gannaway

How Do You Get Alignment?

Whatever your preferred change model that best applies to your current situation, whether it is the Prosci ADKAR model, which says that change is achieved by taking employees through a process of awareness, desire, knowledge, ability, and reinforcement, or Kotter's change management theory, there are key areas that you'll need to work on. Kotter's eight-step process involves creating a sense of urgency, recruiting powerful change leaders, building a vision and effectively communicating it, removing obstacles, creating quick wins, and building on your momentum.

The four key areas to focus on for improved alignment are as follows:

- Understanding the gaps between what you're seeing and what needs to be achieved.

- Building a shared awareness and understanding of corporate strategy and how it applies at a team and individual level.
- Building judgment.
- Constant evaluation that leads to improvement.

Building a Shared Awareness and Understanding

If we rewind to our chapter on the foundations of internal communication and stakeholder mapping, an excellent first step is bringing managers together to see how their worlds connect with others in the organization toward the common corporate strategy. They can also help identify risks and mitigations in the strategy planning stage.

By doing this, you are building a strategy community you can nurture. We're moving on to the second level of our multilayered model—using the network effect across your organization.

Building Judgment

Judgment is built over time through opportunities to practice exercising it. It relies on trust, psychological safety, supported behaviors, and cultural principles. These are all parts of alignment. Building judgment goes beyond just providing information or telling someone how to make good decisions. Here we need to move toward our third level, the experience. It is about interactivity, exploring, and self-motivation. It is about people being empowered to make the right decisions, having the knowledge to make the right decisions, and having the support and psychological safety to occasionally make less-than-ideal decisions and learn from them.

New technology offers ways to practice good judgment. One of the best cases for virtual reality is the training space. Companies such as IKEA, and frontline worker environments such as police departments in Florida and California, have used virtual reality scenario training, helping employees practice difficult situations. I can see this as being a future option for knowledge workers, especially using technology that is AI-powered and that can adapt and learn. It would be a bit like having a virtual mentor.

Evaluation and Improvement

Here we spring back down to our first level, the basics, the foundation. Listening and measurement will help you understand if your team and organizational alignment are improving. The ongoing dialogue throughout your organization will help you know if you are progressing toward better alignment. The ultimate test is, of course, reaching business outcomes that can be directly linked back to the alignment work you've done.

What You'll Get When Aligned

When your team and organization are aligned, you'll get better collaboration between teams, better employee experience, and better employee engagement.

The best way is to ask people for their feedback, and communicate with them, rather than guessing at the answers, which I've seen many leaders unknowingly attempting to do.

It's about creating a shared understanding.

Alexander is the communication leader for an international retailer with both online and shopfront stores. He shared with me that they asked their shopfront staff what tools would most help them. Management was surprised to hear the resounding answer was a pen. The frontline staff needed pens to sign contracts. To fill in paperwork. Alignment and understanding aren't always top-down. In this case, senior management received a better idea of frontline priorities and are now able to make better operational decisions help their frontline people reach company goals.

> ### Questions to Ask to Check Alignment and Stakeholder Engagement
>
> - Are the right people talking?
> - Are the people around me working on projects that directly contribute to our corporate goals? If not, why not?
> - Could I go away on vacation for three months and feel confident that my team will still be directly contributing to corporate goals?

> - How well does our organization support the achievement of our strategy?
> - What support do our people need to have a better, shared understanding?

Case Study: Aligning Competing Company Cultures for a Merger

"Help me help you," is one of Priya Bates's favorite quotes when she consults with leaders, but neither of us could remember which Tom Cruise movie it was from. We laughed. Priya is one of those internal communication celebrities who is warm; generous with her ideas, and makes you feel like you've known them forever. She spoke with me from her office in Ontario, Canada. As president of Inner Strength Communication her love, like mine, is of strategic internal communication. She is also coauthor of *Building a Culture of Inclusivity: Effective Internal Communication for Diversity, Equity, and Inclusion* with UK practitioner Advita Patel.

"Alignment creates trust," Priya said.

> Because if you're saying something and it's not connected to actions, behaviors, and consistent direction, that's when those seeds of distrust are sewed. It's a lot harder when you lose the trust of your employees. That's a lot harder to recover from, to gain the trust back because they are potentially not only your customers but also the people who you rely on to get the job done.

Early on in her career, in her 30s, Priya worked in the integration team for the Hewlett-Packard and Compaq merger, which was one of the largest technology mergers in the early 2000s. She attributes this experience as being foundational to the way she still tackles complex projects, learning from some of the best practices there. The two companies had vastly different cultures.

Priya described to me how it was in an environment of uncertainty—the intent to acquire had been announced on September 3, 2001, and a week later was the infamous September 11, 2001. The two organizations were going through their legal and financial approvals and there were proxy battles—the children of the Hewletts and Packards were opposed to the merger, one leading an effort to make sure the merger didn't go through.

A series of cleanroom teams were created to manage the merger. In these settings, what is spoken in the room stays in the room, which was important as they were to receive confidential information about the two competitors, and there was the possibility that the merger wouldn't go through.

"We were able to say, let's imagine what this organization looks like when it merges," Priya said.

As part of the communications team connected to the HR teams, she was mostly focused on culture, values, and the HR part of the process.

Priya said:

> What do the values look like? We have the cowboys from Compaq, a Houston-based company known for its agility, and then we had Hewlett-Packard, with the great history, really focused on people, but was starting to suffer from bureaucracy. There was such a misalignment between the two cultures. It was an incredible experience to identify what we wanted to leave behind and what the new HP could look like, and prepare the messaging in advance, to have it ready and already be able to start working on the alignment of the culture.
>
> But there were teams who were looking at the alignment of operations, what products were being brought forward, what strategies were being brought forward, where did we want to prioritize our focus? What was the best of the two organizations that we wanted to keep?

A lot of planning went into how the new values and strategies would be launched and how the leaders would be positioned front and center, starting with Cara Carleton "Carly" Fiorina, the CEO of Hewlett-Packard from 1999 to 2005.

The merger happened on May 2, 2002, and was announced through events in the big offices, with Carly speaking from California and broadcasting to all employees.

"But you don't want to launch and leave," Priya said.

You need to see the game play out and I'm a big believer in bite-sized pieces. It's Maslow's hierarchy of needs, right, and you need to address what is the first thing on people's minds. Am I going to have a job? Of course, we're going to talk about who are we as a new company and create some excitement about what that new company looks like. And then we're going to have to deal with who will be part of that new company.

She explained: It had been announced that the merger was going to result in 10 percent layoffs, which when you're thinking about 160,000 people organization globally, that meant 16,000 jobs cut, which is still a relatively significant number to let go. But then people tend to focus on the 10 percent. We chose to focus on the 90 percent. I think that's what we forget during mergers is saying, guess what, folks 9 out of 10 of you are going to still be with us. It was making the case that we want to be part of the new company, and we'd like to bring everyone with us, but unfortunately, that's not going to be the case. But we will let you know as soon as possible, and that started on day one once the leadership decisions were made. So, you knew which leaders were chosen to move forward with the new company and in what capacity and role. And then we started working through the different levels in the organization.

Priya said they took the same approach with the strategy and made sure the context for the different countries, departments, and teams was given. There had been a lot of planning and preparation working closely between the communication and HR teams to work through all of the messaging and information beforehand.

It had taken them approximately six months of preparation and then a few months after the merger to keep things moving until it became business as usual, with her team moving from being a part of the global integration team to a connected, integrated effort with operations, marketing, and branding, to a more operational internal communication role.

Priya's top three tips for merging two cultures and creating strategic alignment to the new culture are as follows:

- Take the time to plan. The planning stage is important as it will help you move forward.
- Remember that the merger is not the end. It is the beginning of the conversation with employees until the new organization is stable and it is business as usual.
- Manage the conversation. Help your people through the change process. They'll go through shock, anger, and resistance. What is the information they need to know to create the stability they want to have again, what is the role that leadership plays?

"Every project is nuanced," Priya said.

If you can't figure out how everything's connected, from your values to the actual behaviors, from the words you're using though the actual actions, from the brand promises you're making to the employee experiences and the customer experiences, then you're not working on the right thing.

Both the leader, internal communication professional, and the whole project team must have a clear understanding of how these are linked.

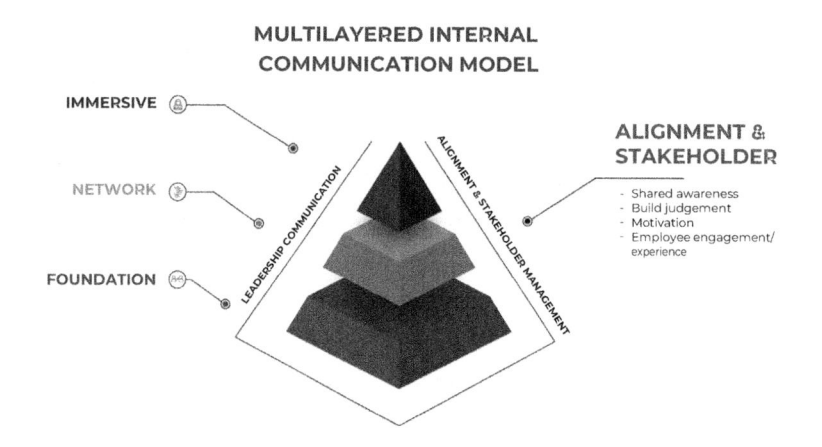

MULTILAYERED INTERNAL COMMUNICATION MODEL

IMMERSIVE

NETWORK

FOUNDATION

LEADERSHIP COMMUNICATION

ALIGNMENT & STAKEHOLDER MANAGEMENT

ALIGNMENT & STAKEHOLDER
- Shared awareness
- Build judgement
- Motivation
- Employee engagement/experience

If you're not aligned with your people and stakeholders, your project is going nowhere.

> **Key Takeaways**
>
> It's the leader's role to make sure the team understands how their daily work contributes to the company's goals and strategy and they are motivated to do so. This is the most crucial factor in leading high-performing teams.
>
> - Alignment isn't just telling someone what to do; it is enabling them to make good decisions.
> - Making sure others have "skin in the game" and want to take responsibility gives better results.
> - There is a positive relationship between employee experience, employee engagement, and employee alignment.
> - Excellent communication is essential to employee motivation and high performance.

CHAPTER 8

Embracing Tomorrow

What Is Your Role in the Future of Communication?

The blades of the lawn were long, lush green, and silky. My cousin Bart from the Netherlands had come to visit us over the weekend with his friends and we were sheltering in the shade of the great, leafy trees at the local park. The weather was typical of a Berlin summer, thunderstorms and rain by night, and hot, sweltering humidity during the day. I could see the sweat beading on Felix's forehead only a few meters from me across the picnic blanket and it made me think of that Melbourne summer. Felix was in public affairs. Wiebke, who was sitting next to him on his hotel towel squished on the grass, was a senior editor of a prominent Dutch news outlet and former journalist. We were in a heated discussion about the impact of AI on any form of content production.

My story of graphic designer Keith's foray into entirely AI-created video with script, voice over, and visuals surfaced. Felix jumped in to discuss framing and arts of persuasion, with the wry revelation that lobbying in his sector still relied on people who were deep into the topic and knew the issues. In his view, "lobbyists for hire" don't cut the mustard. Felix felt that the time taken to train the lobbyists for hire wasn't worth the ultimate time saved by having an extra pair of hands for a short amount of time. This is the same dilemma that every manager faces. Are my team members trained and skilled enough to pick up the task I want to allocate to them if I give them a proper briefing, or is it simply quicker to do it myself? Perhaps training an AI content-generation tool would bring different results. We weren't sure.

From a newsroom perspective, Wiebke shared with us the finding of one of his colleague's research projects into AI-generated photography. His colleague was a photojournalist and had come to the same conclusion as many of us looking forward to what the world with AI could bring in the coming years. While AI was there to spot patterns, make diagnoses, generate ideas, and create artwork, it still needed the human element for quality control and understanding the nuances.

We need a fundamental understanding of what "good" looks like.

I recollected my conversations with experts, such as the senior technical architect at Microsoft Technology Center, Peter Lundig Smith, in March 2023. We talked about how Copilot was designed to work with you, not take you out of the driver's seat. We are still responsible for the results. It can help us, but we are still in control and responsible.

The role of the business leader is not to create the content or even the strategy, but to have the curiosity to ask the right questions to make sure the right audience-centric choices have been made and risks have been considered. It is also important to have one eye on the present, what is happening now, what are the challenges right now, and which stakeholders need more work. The second eye must always be looking to the future and dealing with the challenges to come. These unknown challenges could be everything from skills and resources that will be needed to how to test and trial new ways of communicating, constantly adding to the toolbox, and our own understanding of what works and why.

When I asked Rita Men, American-based practitioner and Director of Internal Communication Research at the University of Florida's College of Journalism and Communication, what her advice to business leaders is, she said "Trust the value of internal communication because it is increasingly critical in today's social media and AI era."

"Embrace the function and just trust your internal communication people, their team, and let them try to demonstrate the value," she advised with a firm nod. "Be open-minded and try new things."

Leadership communication remains the not-so-secret weapon of any leader. Done well, it can not only bring success to an internal communication campaign but also professionally help the leader with their positioning both within and external to an organization. A leader who is not only positioned well but who can also consistently communicate well will be able to more effectively persuade and help others to want to follow them. They will be equipped with more business intelligence simply because they have listened to their people.

It is important to invest in strategic internal communication. This book has shown how important it is, that internal communication is a strategic business function, and not a tactical one.

Your Multilayered Toolbox for Internal Communication

As a fellow communicator once said to me, a communication toolbox is like having a backpack. Wherever you are, whatever role or project you are working with, you can slip your backpack off your shoulders and plonk it on the ground. Roll out your swag and set up quickly, ready to go, with little fuss. The organizations might change, and the target audiences and stakeholders are likely different, but the principles, tools, and techniques are the same. You just need to choose the right ones for each situation.

With my multilayered toolbox, there are now three key levels when selecting your communication tactics: foundational, network, and immersive communication. Running throughout internal communication and holding it together is leadership communication and strategic alignment—making sure you're all pulling and pushing together, or at least working in the same direction.

Curiosity and consultancy skills are the two skills that should always be nurtured in communication teams. With the increasing ease of content production, we leave ourselves open to risk when we fail to question the facts. Without questioning processes, we risk being left behind with old ways of doing things, where the internal communication professional is the order taker, or the cookie-cutter campaign strategy is the status quo, despite changes in the environment, message, or target audience. Without curiosity, our communication professionals also have no hope of remaining current with new digital opportunities. Technology will keep changing faster than imaginable.

Looking at the Technology Landscape

Although technology can be a shiny new toy, it will always remain a tool or channel to achieve a specific result for communication within our organizations.

Best practice is for IT, HR, and internal communication to work together in selecting the right technology mix for your people. A channel strategy needs to be built and clearly identify the purpose for each channel. Too many different chat options, collaboration tools, and ways of communicating with one another will likely confuse people and they won't know where to look for information or the best way to reach specific colleagues. A channel strategy should focus on all channels that a company uses, including ones external to the company that staff use, such as social media.

For every major technology change, internal communication will be needed to bring people on board, help inspire them to the new ways of working, get them to use the new technology, and share their learnings with others. Don't underestimate the value of a good adoption campaign, and at the heart of this are all of the concepts we've discussed throughout.

AI brings so many new ways to be more productive and streamlined within organizations and it will continue, along with other technology, to shape the way internal communication is done.

The internal communication team can benefit from looking at their own work processes and then helping the rest of the organization to get on board with the change.

What we want to avoid is technology inequality—where some people are left behind because they are not supported in the change.

Overview: How to Get Your Internal Communication Team Started With Using AI

Some of the ways AI can help a communication team include the following:

- Data crunching and admin (but the data has to be good).
- Ideation for content (but you need to know what prompts to use).
- Content creation (and you need to know what good looks like).
- Fresh eyes (checking editing, grammar suggestions, applying tone of voice, giving brand suggestions, and sharpening communication).

- Organizational listening (sentiment analysis, pulling data, and analyzing facial expressions).
- Language translation.

It helps when the individual team members start with their own imagination about what could help them in their role; they feel supported by their team; there's great resources, and they have the expectations of their stakeholders around them managed.

GETTING COMFORTABLE WITH AI

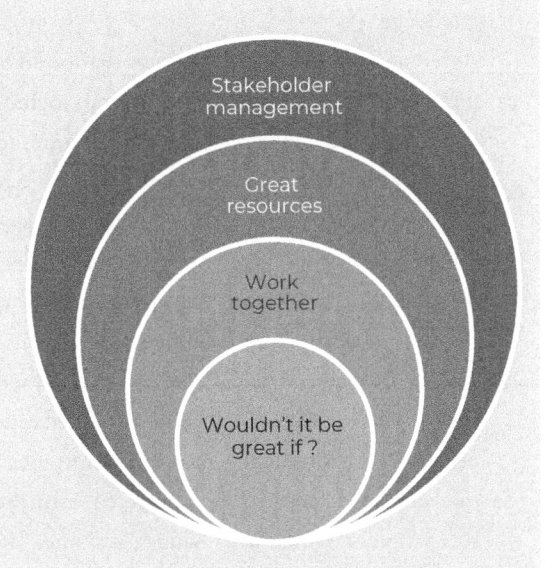

- Stakeholder management
- Great resources
- Work together
- Wouldn't it be great if?

A high-level process for deliberately incorporating more AI into the way that internal communication is run in your organization could look like this:

1) Know your company policies on AI use.
2) Create a baseline understanding of everyone affected through a workshop or training session.
3) Get employees to identify their pain points in their roles and imagine where AI could help them (self-motivation).
4) Agree on an ideal vision.
5) A smaller taskforce or champions will need to:
   a) Map existing workflows
   b) Collaborate with technical specialists to do the research on what products are available to your organization, what other

organizations use for those tasks, and what would best fit your needs.
c) Make recommendations and propose new ways of working and identify any specific training needed for the users.
d) Be digital literacy experts (syntax) and study prompt engineering.
e) Regularly share knowledge with the team.

6) Encourage the team to play with new AI tools and share. Offer extra training or support to those who need it. Set a 100-day challenge.

7) Agree on any necessary guidelines that build on your company AI policies. For example, is it necessary to include disclaimers on the work, is it okay to change people's appearance beyond enhancement? What checks and balances are in place for the team to make sure a human reviews the work before it goes out?

8) Create a transition plan with the team, identifying costs, timelines, specific goals, and helping to identify quick wins. What is needed for this plan to be successful?

9) Keep your project manager for the transition plan accountable, making sure they review priorities regularly, check in with the users that AI is reducing time and improving results. The project manager also needs to be connected with the company big-picture IT plans, which will change over time. The new processes will need to be documented for people joining the team or as the processes change. For example, where will the prompt cheat-sheets for the team be kept?

10) Celebrate and share wins with and beyond the team. Always manage upward and outward.

Bringing Culture to Life

As technology allows us to connect more effectively across the globe and work becomes more human-centric with flexible working hours, locations, and commitments, bringing culture to life through internal communication and supporting others to do so is an important counterbalance to the push for technology. The company culture emerges through every interaction, every message, every sign of listening, and every moment of communication.

Leaders Like You Care About Effective Communication

I reflect back on my conversation with Sean, such a long time ago, across the world in that dry Melbourne heat, on the balcony of a fancy city café. We'd talked about what AI would bring to the communication world and our organization. How all the areas of business need to work together to develop solutions that work for people.

Since then we couldn't have possibly imagined how fast technology and AI has leapt ahead, and no one quite knows where it will go. Instead of life and communication becoming simpler, it seems they have become more complex, with interwoven possibilities, multigenerational, and cultural overlays.

I wonder what answers I would give Sean now? How will we see the landscape in a year's time, or will this AI thing fade into an everyday norm?

Yet the one thing that remains constant is people. People are complex. And without human interaction and without effective communication we cannot work toward the same goals, whether it is a business goal or a societal goal. Communication is a skill that can be learned and improved upon, and effective internal communication at scale has been proven to lead to business success.

Gather your partners in crime or tribe, however, you like to think of your allies, and go create something amazing with them.

Inspire them, engage with them, and give them ownership to continue to be a part of and understand your organization. Don't be boring, be fun, engaging, bold, and push the boundaries.

The choice is yours. It's up to you.

Key Takeaways

Communicating effectively at scale within an organization is powerful and is an essential tool for leadership and business success, regardless of what technology is available.

- People come first. Technology merely enables.
- In the age of AI, asking the right questions and having a sense of what "good" communication looks like is essential for wisely managing budgets and protecting staff from information overload.
- The internal communication strategy should be customized to the audience, the level of complexity of what you're trying to achieve, and the budget of time, money, and resources that you're willing to spend.
- Never skimp on stakeholder engagement.
- Alignment is essential for success.
- Be curious, think creatively, and embrace the future.

Bibliography

Introduction

"Internal Communication Research Hub Research." n.d. *UF College of Journalism and Communications*. www.jou.ufl.edu/icrh-research/ (accessed October 24, 2023).

Mo Gawdat: AI Today, Tomorrow and How You Can Save Our World. October 2, 2023. Nordic Business Forum 2023. www.youtube.com/watch?v=u9CEUzH4HL4 (accessed October 14, 2023).

"Word—Microsoft Translator for Business." 2018. *Microsoft Translator for Business*. www.microsoft.com/en-us/translator/business/word/ (accessed October 20, 2023).

Bailey, R. September 25, 2023. "Briefing: AI in PR." PR Academy. https://pracademy.co.uk/insights/briefing-ai-in-pr/.

Harvard Business Review. May 11, 2023. "Why Overhauling Internal Communications Could Be Your Greatest Revenue Driver." https://hbr.org/sponsored/2023/05/why-overhauling-internal-communications-could-be-your-greatest-revenue-driver (accessed July 23, 2023).

Miller, R. 2024. "Chapter 2." *Internal Communication Strategy: Design, Develop and Transform Your Organizational Communication*. Kogan Page.

Miller, R. September 8, 2020. "How to Prove the Value of Communication." *All Things IC*. www.allthingsic.com/how-to-prove-the-value-of-communication/ (accessed October 20, 2023).

Rowley, J. October 11, 2023. "Review of LLM Benchmarks: Guide to Evaluating Language Models." *Deepgram*. https://deepgram.com/learn/llm-benchmarks-guide-to-evaluating-language-models.

State of the Sector 2022/2023. 2023. London: Gallagher. www.ajg.com/employeeexperience/-/media/files/gallaghercomms/gcommssite/state-of-the-sector-2023.pdf (accessed May 8, 2023).

Step Two. n.d. "Review of Christy Punch, Wells Fargo (USA), Using Cutting-Edge Microservices to Go beyond the Fundamentals." www.steptwo.com.au/speaker/christy-punch/ (accessed September 21, 2023).

Chapter 1

"Natural Language Generation—Turn Data Into Words With Arria NLG." n.d. Arria NLG. /www.arria.com/ (accessed October 24, 2023).

BIBLIOGRAPHY

"We Are Hearken." n.d. *Hearken*. https://wearehearken.com/ (accessed October 24, 2023).

Arvanitis, L., M. Sadeghi, and J. Brewster. March 2023. "Review of Despite OpenAI's Promises, the Company's New AI Tool Produces Misinformation More Frequently, and More Persuasively, than Its Predecessor." *NewsGuard*. www.newsguardtech.com/misinformation-monitor/march-2023.

Chesky, B. May 5, 2020. "Review of a Message From Co-Founder and CEO Brian Chesky." Airbnb. https://news.airbnb.com/a-message-from-co-founder-and-ceo-brian-chesky/.

Cohn, L. and R. Marty. February 2, 2023. "Review of a Journey to the Metaverse-Office Frontier." *Gartner Business Quarterly*. www.gartner.com/document/4049399. ID G00783888.

CrowdTangle. n.d. *CrowdTangle | Content Discovery and Social Monitoring Made Easy*. www.crowdtangle.com/.

Descript. 2023 *Descript | Create Podcasts, Videos, and Transcripts*. www.descript.com.

European Parliament. March 13, 2024. "Artificial Intelligence Act: MEPs Adopt Landmark Lw." Press release. www.europarl.europa.eu/news/en/press-room/20240308IPR19015/artificial-intelligence-act-meps-adopt-landmark-law#:~:text=On%20Wednesday%2C%20Parliament%20approved%20the,46%20against%20and%2049%20abstentions.

Field, J. August 31, 2022. "Council Post: Why We Need to Stop Confusing Employee Engagement and Internal Communication." *Forbes*. www.forbes.com/sites/forbesbusinesscouncil/2022/08/31/why-we-need-to-stop-confusing-employee-engagement-and-internal-communication (accessed March 16, 2023).

FitzPatrick, L. and K. Valskov. 2014. *Internal Communications: A Manual for Practitioners*. London: Kogan Page.

Garante per La Protezione Dei Dati Personali GDP 2023. March 31, 2023. "Review of Intelligenza Artificiale: Il Garante Blocca ChatGPT." www.garanteprivacy.it/web/guest/home/docweb/-/docweb-display/docweb/9870847. Translated using Google Translate.

Gartner Communications Research Team. February 20, 2023. "Review of Information Overload and the Future of Internal Communications." *Gartner*. www.gartner.com/document/4102099.

Geuter, J. September 25, 2023. "Letter to Monqiue Zytnik." *Email*.

Hashim, D. December 24, 2022. "Review of Sketching the Field of AI Tools for Local Newsrooms." *Medium*. Partnership on AI. https://medium.com/partnership-on-ai/sketching-the-field-of-ai-tools-for-local-newsrooms-62e9d0620eb5.

Henke, S., A. Ringsted, and M. Zytnik. 2022. "Review of Steffen Henke and Andreas Ringsted on the Relationship Between Technology and Internal

Communication Podcast." *IABC EMENA SoundCloud.* https://soundcloud.com/user-687327695/steffen-henke-and-andreas-ringsted-on-the-relationship-between-technology-and-internal-communication.

Klein, L.K., E. Earl, and D. Cundick. May 1, 2023. "Reducing Information Overload in Your Organization." *Harvard Business Review.* https://hbr.org/2023/05/reducing-information-overload-in-your-organization.

Klein, M. January 31, 2023. "Call with Monique Zytnik." *2023 Video.*

Mauran, C. April 6, 2023. "Whoops, Samsung Workers Accidentally Leaked Trade Secrets Via ChatGPT." *Mashable.* https://mashable.com/article/samsung-chatgpt-leak-details.

McKinsey. June 14, 2023. *Economic Potential of Generative AI | McKinsey.* www.mckinsey.com. www.mckinsey.com/capabilities/mckinsey-digital/our-insights/the-economic-potential-of-generative-ai-the-next-productivity-frontier#business-value.

Metz, C. and K. Weise. October 16, 2023. "How 'A.I. Agents' That Roam the Internet Could One Day Replace Workers." *The New York Times.* sec. Technology. www.nytimes.com/2023/10/16/technology/ai-agents-workers-replace.html.

Millington, E., H. Sarekanno, M. Mason, M. Crosby, T. Barker, M. Crosby, R, Tsehay, and S. Holten. 2023. *IC 2023 Index: The Voice of UK Employees Helping to Inform Strategic Choices Across Internal Communication.* Institute of Internal Communication.

Phillips, T. 2020. *Truth: A Brief History of Total Bullsh*T.* London: Wildfire.

State of the Sector 2022/2023. 2023. London: Gallagher. www.ajg.com/employeeexperience/-/media/files/gallaghercomms/gcommssite/state-of-the-sector-2023.pdf (accessed May 8, 2023).

Vince. n.d. *LLM Benchmark. LL Monitor.* https://benchmarks.llmonitor.com/sally (accessed September 27, 2023).

Chapter 2

Digital Communications Awards 2021. n.d. "Winner List 2021." www.digital-awards.eu/best-of-2021 (accessed September 20, 2023).

Grunig, J.E. and J.-N. Kim. September 2021. *Review of the Four Models of Public Relations and Their Research Legacy.* www.researchgate.net/profile/James-Grunig/publication/349183517_15_The_four_models_of_public_relations_and_their_research_legacy/links/614f4e1a154b3227a8acd40e/15-The-four-models-of-public-relations-and-their-research-legacy.pdf.

Trevor, J. and B. Varcoe. September 21, 2017. "How Aligned Is Your Organization?" *Harvard Business Review.* https://hbr.org/2017/02/how-aligned-is-your-organization.

Zytnik, M. and M. Lequick. 2024. "Review of Getting Colleagues Comfortable With AI: A Human-Centered Approach to Technology in Organizations."

In *Public Relations and Communications: Cases, Reflections, and Predictions*, ed. A. Adi. Berlin: Quadriga University. www.quadriga-hochschule.com/app/uploads/2023/09/QHS_Artificial_Intelligence_in_Public_Relations__Communications_2023.pdf.

Chapter 3

AMEC. n.d. "Evaluation of the Pink Sari Project—Multicultural Health Communication Service—AMEC | International Association for the Measurement and Evaluation of Communication." https://amecorg.com/case-study/evaluation-of-the-pink-sari-project-multicultural-health-communication-service/ (accessed August 2, 2023).

Benson, F. and A. Reid. May 25, 2023. *Interview by Monique Zytnik*.

Cowan, D. 2017. *Strategic Internal Communication: How to Build Employee Engagement and Performance*. 2nd ed. London. Kogan Page Ltd.

Emergence. 2018. "Rise of the Deskless Workforce." http://desklessworkforce2018.com. (accessed July 15, 2023).

Field, J. 2021. *Influential Internal Communication: Streamline Your Corporate Communication to Drive Efficiency and Engagement*. New York, NY: Kogan Page Inc. Table 1.1.

Institute of Internal Communication. September 12, 2023. "Review of AI and the Future of Internal Communication." Milton Keynes, United Kingdom: IoIC and The Future of Work. www.ioic.org.uk/resource-report/ai-and-the-future-of-internal-communication.html (accessed September 24, 2023).

Kruse, K. June 26, 2015. "What Is Employee Engagement." *Forbes*. www.forbes.com/sites/kevinkruse/2012/06/22/employee-engagement-what-and-why/.

O'Sullivan, D. and C. Duffy. November 4, 2022. "Elon Musk's Twitter Lays Off Employees Across the Company | CNN Business." *CNN*. https://edition.cnn.com/2022/11/03/tech/twitter-layoffs/index.html.

Panetta, K. March 2017. "Review of a CIO's Framework for Communicating Strategy." *Gartner*. www.gartner.com/smarterwithgartner/a-cios-framework-for-communicating-strategy.

Pounsford, M. and H. Krais. March 27, 2023. *Interview by Monique Zytnik*.

Chapter 4

De Smet, A., B. Dowling, B. Hancock, and B. Schaninger. July 13, 2022. "The Great Renegotiation and New Talent Pools | McKinsey." www.mckinsey.com. www.mckinsey.com/capabilities/people-and-organizational-performance/our-insights/the-great-attrition-is-making-hiring-harder-are-you-searching-the-right-talent-pools.

BIBLIOGRAPHY

Godin, S. 2008. *Tribes We Need You to Lead Us.* London: Penguin Books.

Leonardi, P. and T. Neeley. November–December, 2017. "Review of What Managers Need to Know about Social Tools." *Harvard Business Review Magazine.* https://hbr.org/2017/11/what-managers-need-to-know-about-social-tools (accessed March 3, 2023).

Lock Lee, L. and S. Dawson. 2023. "Review of Swoop Analytics 2022/23 Yammer & Viva Engage Benchmarking Report." *Swoop Analytics.* https://swooppublic.blob.core.windows.net/publicfiles/Benchmarking%20reports/Yammer/2022/SWOOP-Yammer-BM-2022-23.pdf (accessed March 3, 2023).

Mortensen, M. and A.C. Edmondson. January 1, 2023. "Rethink Your Employee Value Proposition." *Harvard Business Review.* https://hbr.org/2023/01/rethink-your-employee-value-proposition.

PlaySide Studios and Dumb Ways to Die. August 2, 2023. "Review of Dumb Ways to Die." www.dumbwaystodie.com/psa (accessed August 2, 2023).

Thackeray, R. and B.L. Neiger. 2009. "A Multidirectional Communication Model: Implications for Social Marketing Practice." *Health Promotion Practice* 10, no. 2, pp. 171175. https://doi.org/10.1177/1524839908330729.

Vandor, P., L. Leitner, R. Miller, and H. Hansen. 2020. "Review of Addressing Grand Challenges Collectively: An Introduction to Impact-Orientated Networks." Berlin: IAC Berlin and Social Entrepreneurship Center Vienna University of Economics and Business. www.linkedin.com/in/tobias-gerber-a6a1638b/overlay/1613394748774/single-media-viewer/?type=DOCUMENT&profileId=ACoAABMQ_DIBj6Bsy2SuVgIXVUX-G-OXDC_tZ10 (accessed March 1, 2023).

Wiener-Bronner, D. April 20, 2023. "Anheuser-Busch Facilities Face Threats After Bud Light Backlash | CNN Business." *CNN.* https://edition.cnn.com/2023/04/20/business/bud-light-threats/index.html.

Windley, D. June 24, 2022 "Council Post: The Value of Employer Branding." *Forbes.* www.forbes.com/sites/forbeshumanresourcescouncil/2022/06/24/the-value-of-employer-branding/.

Zytnik, M. 2019. *Review of Learning to Laugh: Using Humour to Cut Through and Strengthen Engagement.* www.slideshare.net/MoniqueZytnik1/learning-to-laugh-using-humour-to-cut-through-and-strengthen-employee-engagement-178648269.

Chapter 5

"Digital Scent Technologies Market Top Companies | Digital Scent Technologies Industry Trends by 2028." April 20, 2023. *Emergen Research.* www.emergenresearch.com/blog/top-7-leading-companies-advancing-digital-scent-technologies (accessed August 3, 2023).

Ching-Chiuan, Y. 2023. "Review of Digital Flavour." *Keio-NUS Connective Ubiquitous Technology for Embodiments, National University of Singapore.* https://cutecenter.nus.edu.sg/projects/digital-flavor.html (accessed August 3, 2023).

Ching-Chiuan, Y. August 6. 2023. *Email with Monique Zytnik.*

Diaz, J. 2021. *The Secrets of LEGO House.* San Francisco: Chronicle Books.

Markenklang | BVG Unternehmen. 2022. "Review of Ganz Berlin wird Ohren machen!" https://unternehmen.bvg.de/markenklang (accessed August 3, 2023).

NUS News Writers. July 28, 2023. "A Review of a Training Boost for Traffic Accident and Hazmat Emergency Responders Through Extended Reality." *National University of Singapore.* https://news.nus.edu.sg/training-boost-for-emergency-responders-through-xr (accessed August 8, 2023).

NUS News Writers. October 14, 2019. "Review of NUS Team Creates Interactive, Multisensory VR Game." National University of Singapore. https://news.nus.edu.sg/research/nus-team-creates-interactive-multisensory-vr-game (accessed August 8, 2023).

Purdy, M., M. Klymenko, and M. Purdy. May 3, 2021. "Business Scents: The Rise of Digital Olfaction." *MIT Sloan Management Review.* https://sloanreview.mit.edu/article/business-scents-the-rise-of-digital-olfaction/ (accessed August 3, 2023).

Stokes, R. November 6, 2015. "Review of Gamification Is Exciting because It Promises to Make the Hard Stuff in Life Fun." *LinkedIn.* www.linkedin.com/pulse/gamification-exciting-because-promises-make-hard-stuff-richard-stokes/ (accessed August 3, 2023).

Wu, T. 2017. *The Attention Merchants: The Epic Scramble to Get inside Our Heads.* New York, NY: Vintage Books.

Chapter 6

Avery, J. and R. Greenwald. May 1, 2023. "A New Approach to Building Your Personal Brand." *Harvard Business Review.* https://hbr.org/2023/05/a-new-approach-to-building-your-personal-brand.

Brown, B. 2018. "Dare to Lead: Brave Work." *Tough Conversations. Whole Hearts,* p. 222. London: Vermilion/Random House.

Burgund, H. and F. Panetta. n.d. *In Event of Moon Disaster—Home.* https://moondisaster.org/.

Corden, J. July 21, 2016. "Review of First Lady Michelle Obama Carpool Karaoke Video." *The Late Show With James Corden YouTube.* www.youtube.com/watch?v=ln3wAdRAim4 (accessed September 22, 2023).

Gallo, C. 2019. *Five Stars: The Communication Secrets to Get From Good to Great.* New York, NY: St. Martin's Griffin.

Gallo, C. November 23, 2022. "How Great Leaders Communicate." *Harvard Business Review*. https://hbr.org/2022/11/how-great-leaders-communicate.

Godin, S. 2020. "Review of Seth Godin: Authenticity Is Overrated. Here's What You Need Instead Video." *YouTube*. www.youtube.com/watch?v=lbJtuaFebtA.

Harris, T. and A. Raskin. 2023. "Review of the A.I. Dilemma—9 March 2023." *YouTube Video*. www.youtube.com/watch?v=xoVJKj8lcNQ.

Holdforth, L. 2019. *Leading Lines: How to Make Speeches That Seize the Moment, Advance Your Cause and Lead the Way*. Sydney: HarperCollins.

Macaulay, K. and J. Anthoine. April 5, 2023. "Episode 78—Comms With Courage." *Podcast*. https://abcomm.co.uk/podcasts/episode/episode-78-comms-with-courage (accessed April 14, 2023).

MIT Open Learning. July 20, 2020. "Review of Tackling the Misinformation Epidemic With 'in Event of Moon Disaster'. Massachusetts Institute of Technology. https://news.mit.edu/2020/mit-tackles-misinformation-in-event-of-moon-disaster-0720.

Morrow, A. April 20, 2023. "CEO Apologizes After 'Pity City' Speech Backfires | CNN Business." *CNN*. https://edition.cnn.com/2023/04/20/business/pity-city-ceo-apologizes/index.html.

NBC News YouTube. April 20, 2023. "Review of MillerKnoll CEO Says to "Leave Pity City" in Meeting on Company Performance." *Video*. www.youtube.com/watch?v=2EttMDA0gRk.

PBS News Hour YouTube. March 8, 2016. "Review of Watch Michelle Obama Speak on International Women's Day." *Video*. https://youtu.be/FIN1F0TyadM.

Rosner, D. May 17, 2023. *Video interview With Monique Zytnik*.

Sharp-Paul, N. 2021. "Review of Changing Communication in a Changing World." In *The IABC Guide for Practical Business Communication: A Global Standard Primer*, ed. T. Gillis, 101. Chicago: IABC.

Whitworth, B. 2021. "Review of Leading the Communications Function." In *The IABC Guide for Practical Business Communication: A Global Standard Primer*, ed. T. Gillis, 71. Chicago: IABC.

Chapter 7

"The 22 Best Examples of How Companies Use Virtual Reality for Training." n.d. *Full-Service vr & AR Agency*. www.vrowl.io/the-22-best-examples-of-how-companies-use-virtual-reality-for-training/.

Gannaway, B. and E. Bridger. 2024. *Employee Experience by Design—How to Create an Effective EX for Competitive Advantage*. 2nd ed. Kogan Page.

Sinek, S. 2020. *The Infinite Game*. London: Portfolio Penguin.

Voss, C. 2017. *Never Split the Difference: Negotiating as If Your Life Depended on It*. London: Random House Business Books.

Trevor, J. and B. Varcoe. May 16, 2016. "A Simple Way to Test Your Company's Strategic Alignment." *Harvard Business Review*. https://hbr.org/2016/05/a-simple-way-to-test-your-companys-strategic-alignment.

Wiles, J. November 4, 2019. "Review of 3 Ways to Keep Managers Aligned With Corporate Strategy." *Gartner*. www.gartner.com/smarterwithgartner/3-ways-keep-managers-aligned-corporate-strategy.

Artis, Z. and M. Zytnik. June 6, 2022. "Review of Organizational, Leadership and Team Alignment With Zora Artis Podcast." *IABC EMENA SoundCloud*. https://soundcloud.com/user-687327695/organisational-leadership-and-team-alignment-with-zora-artis.

Leike, J., J. Schulman, and J. Wu. August 24, 2022. "Our Approach to Alignment Research." *OpenAI*. https://openai.com/blog/our-approach-to-alignment-research.

Communications Research Team. February 24, 2023. "Review of How to Strengthen Employees' Brand Alignment ID G00774504." *Gartner*.

Walsh, M. August 3, 2023. *Audio Interview With Monique Zytnik*.

Chapter 8

Gartner Communications Research Team. November 23, 2022. "Review of How to Leverage Experiential Learning to Improve New Leader Communications." *Gartner*. ID G00745441.

Men, R. September 29, 2023. *Video Interview With Monique Zytnik*.

About the Author

Monique Zytnik is an award-winning, global internal communication leader based in Berlin, Germany.

She has worked internationally, presented on best-practice communication at world conferences, and guest lectured at universities. Her campaigns have been recognized by Gartner, Mubmrella CommsCon, and the Digital Communication Awards. She regularly shares her knowledge through communication industry publications and podcasts, drawing on her in-house and consultancy work with organizations including SBS Radio Australia, The Australian Taxation Office, ANZ Bank, DHL Group, Adjust GmbH, and LEGO Foundation.

Her decades of experience are supported by a Master in Communication (PR) with honors from RMIT University. She gives back to the community by mentoring others through The Mentoring Club and Global Women in Public Relations (GWPR). She is the International Association of Business Communicators (IABC) EMENA Region Chair 2024/25.

Index

Accessibility, 52–53
Alignment, 29–30, 122–124
Artificial intelligence (AI)
  age of, xxviii–xxix
  and internal communication,
    16–18, 134–136
  organizational communication,
    xxxix–xli
Artis, Z., 117–119
Audience analysis, 40–44, 92–93
Audience-centric communication,
  27–28
Augmented reality (AR), 77–79, 85
Authenticity, 99–101

Barnard, C., 57–58
Bates, P., 125–128
Benson, F., 42
Berliner Verkehrsbetriebe (BVG), 89–90
Berlo, D., 26, 38
Bezos, J., 105
Business leader, xxxiii–xxxiv

Cawthra, F., 62
Chartered Institute of Public
    Relations (CIPR), xxxix
ChatGPT, xxviii, 1–5
Chesky, B., 10
Communication
  accessibility, 52–53
  audience-centric, 27–28
  cascade, 55–56
  corporate, 7–8, 16, 52, 63, 89,
    112, 118
  dialogue-based, 26
  employee, 16, 17, 23, 25, 49, 64,
    78, 94
  experience, 48–49
  future of, 131–133
  measurement, 49–50, 52
  nonlinear, 86–87
  risk mitigation, 52
  strategy, 11–14, 31–32

  streamlining, 8–9, 48–49
  See also Internal communication;
    Leadership communication
Community building, 69–73
Consistency, 109
Consultancy skills, 133
Corporate communication, 7–8, 16,
  52, 63, 89, 112, 118
Covid-19 pandemic, 10, 22–23, 27,
  68, 84, 91–93, 102
Curiosity, 133

DHL Virtual Strategy House, 23, 81
Dialogue-based communication, 26
Dixon, M., 80, 90

Effective change and transformation,
  7, 8
Employee alignment, 121
Employee communications, 16, 17,
  23, 25, 49, 64, 78, 94
Employee engagement, 56, 121
Employee experience, 17, 41, 79, 118,
  120–122, 124, 128
Employer branding, 67–69
Enterprise social networks (ESNs),
  48, 63–64, 66–67, 71, 72

FitzPatrick, L., xxix

Gamification, 88
Gannaway, B., 120–122
Gates, B., 24
Gawdat, M., xl–xli
Generative AI (GenAI), xxviii, xl,
  1–2, 10, 117
Geuter, J., 3
Godin, S., 23–24, 57, 65–66, 99–100

Henke, S., 16–18, 118
Holdforth, L., 107
Holtz, S., xli–xlii
Human-centric approach, 57–60

Immersive communication, 22–23, 25, 27–28, 68, 77, 79–83, 85–92
  3D space, 21–22, 77, 81, 85–92
Immersive technology, 6, 25, 77–79, 81–83, 95
Implementation plan, 53–54
Interactive communication, 87–88
Internal communication, xxix–xxxi, 3–6
  affective impact, xxxi
  AI and, 16–18, 134–136
  behavioral impact of, xxxi–xxxii
  professionals, xxxiv–xxxvii
  strategy, 10, 27, 28, 30–31, 44, 79
  value of, 7–9

Judgment, building, 123

Klein, M., xlii
Krais, H., 46–48

Leadership communication, 28–29, 104–109
  sound in, 111–113
  strength, 106–107
  transformational leaders, 103–104
  trust and authenticity, 99–103
Leadership positioning, 106
LLM Benchmark, 4

Macnamara, J., 50–51, 83
Men, R., xxx–xxxiii, 132
Miller, R., xxxiv–xxxv
Multidirectional communication theory, 26–27, 88
Multilayered internal communication model, 29–31, 133

Networks and communities, 64–66
  employer branding, 67–69
  high-functioning, 65
  principles of, 66–69
Nonlinear communication, 86–87

Organizational communication, xxxix–xli
  professional, xxix–xxxi
Organizational culture, 33–35

Organizational listening, 7, 8, 46–48

Pounsford, M., 46–48
Prakash, B., 111–113

RACI analysis, 44–45
Reputation, xxxii–xxxiii
Ringsted, A., xxii, xli, 22–23, 81
Risk mitigation, 52
Rosener, D., 105–106

Sender, Message, Channel, Receiver (SMCR). *See* Dialogue-based communication
Sender–receiver model, 6, 23, 37–39, 43, 56–58
Senses
  smell, 90–92
  sound, 89–90
  taste, 92
  touch, 90
Smell, 90–92
Social media, 6, 14, 25–27, 41, 61, 70–72, 101–102, 134
Sound, 89–90
Stakeholder alignment and management, 29
Stakeholder management, xxxv, 44–45
Storytelling, 108–109
Strategic alignment, 93, 104, 117–121
Strategic thinking, 13–14
Streamlining communication, 8–9, 48–49

Taste, 92
Technology revolution, xxxvii–xxxix, 1–2
Thayer, L., 26
Touch, 90
Transformational leaders, 103–104
Trust, 99–103

Virtual reality (VR), 21–22, 25, 77–79, 91
Viva Engage/Yammer, 34, 63, 73, 74

Walters, D., 58–59

OTHER TITLES IN THE CORPORATE COMMUNICATION COLLECTION

Debbie DuFrene, Stephen F. Austin State University, Editor

- *Ensuring Civility Online* by Virginia Hemby
- *Win Business with Relationships* by May Hongmei Gao
- *Technical Marketing Communication, Second Edition* by Emil B. Towner and Heidi L. Everett
- *The Thong Principle* by Donalee Moulton
- *How to Become a Master of Persuasion* by Tony Treacy
- *101 Tips for Improving Your Business Communication* by Edward Barr
- *Business Writing For Innovators and Change-Makers* by Dawn Henwood
- *Delivering Effective Virtual Presentations* by K. Virginia Hemby
- *New Insights into Prognostic Data Analytics in Corporate Communication* by Pragyan Rath and Kumari Shalini
- *Leadership Through A Screen* by Joseph Brady and Garry Prentice
- *Managerial Communication for Professional Development* by Reginald L. Bell and Jeanette S. Martin
- *Managerial Communication for Organizational Development* by Reginald L. Bell and Jeanette S. Martin

Concise and Applied Business Books

The Collection listed above is one of 30 business subject collections that Business Expert Press has grown to make BEP a premiere publisher of print and digital books. Our concise and applied books are for...

- Professionals and Practitioners
- Faculty who adopt our books for courses
- Librarians who know that BEP's Digital Libraries are a unique way to offer students ebooks to download, not restricted with any digital rights management
- Executive Training Course Leaders
- Business Seminar Organizers

Business Expert Press books are for anyone who needs to dig deeper on business ideas, goals, and solutions to everyday problems. Whether one print book, one ebook, or buying a digital library of 110 ebooks, we remain the affordable and smart way to be business smart. For more information, please visit www.businessexpertpress.com, or contact sales@businessexpertpress.com.

Printed in Great Britain
by Amazon